Integrated
Skills
Reinforcement

**Longman Series in
College Composition and Communication**

Advisory Editor: Harvey Wiener
LaGuardia Community College
The City University of New York

READING, WRITING,
SPEAKING, AND LISTENING
ACROSS THE CURRICULUM

Integrated
Skills
Reinforcement

JOANN ROMEO ANDERSON, *DIRECTOR, ISR PROJECT*
NORA EISENBERG
JOHN HOLLAND
HARVEY S. WIENER
With **CAROL RIVERA-KRON**

An outgrowth of a project in faculty development at Fiorello
H. LaGuardia Community College of the City University of
New York— a project supported, in part, by grants from the
New York State Education Department under the Voca-
tional Education Act, and the U.S. Office of Education
under the Strengthening Developing Institutions Program,
Title III.

Longman
New York & London

Integrated Skills Reinforcement
Reading, Writing, Speaking, and
Listening Across the Curriculum

Longman Inc., 1560 Broadway, New York, N.Y. 10036
Associated companies, branches, and representatives
throughout the world.

Developmental Editor: Gordon T. R. Anderson
Editorial and Design Supervisor: Joan Matthews
Production Supervisor: Ferne Y. Kawahara
Manufacturing Supervisor: Marion Hess

Library of Congress Cataloging in Publication Data
Main entry under title:

Integrated skills reinforcement.

   (Longman series in college composition and communication)
   Includes index.
   1. English language—Study and teaching (Higher)
2. Language arts (Higher)   I. Anderson, JoAnn Romeo.
II. Series.
PE1065.I56   1983   428'.007'1173   82-17124
ISBN 0-582-28238-1

Manufactured in the United States of America
Printing: 9 8 7 6 5 4 3 2 1   Year: 91 90 89 88 87 86 85 84 83

Contents

v

Acknowledgments

Many people have contributed a great deal of thought, creativity, and support to the development of the materials and the model of faculty development suggested in this book. First, we would like to thank all the faculty who have participated in the Integrated Skills Reinforcement (ISR) program over the past five years, the program that laid the foundation for this book. They asked difficult questions of us, of themselves, and of the teaching process; they acknowledged what they did not know and shared what they did. Special thanks to Jeffrey Davis, Ingrid De Cicco, Mary Beth Early, Nicholas Gilroy, George Groman, and Olga Vega for their contributions to the Learning Guide Sampler at the end of this text and thanks to Tony Giangrasso for his guide in statistics that we present as a model of integrated skills reinforcement. Thanks also to Mary Lee Abkemeier, Peter Brown, Betty Farber, Marguerita Grecco, Naomi Greenberg, Howard Kellogg, and Eleanor Q. Tignor for their many creative suggestions and their examples of materials included in this text. Thanks also to Ana Maria Hernandez, Joyce Rheuban, Frank Timoni, and Hannalynn Wilkens. To Jim Weaver, we are grateful for his helpful comments and suggestions on many strategies and particularly for his assistance in thinking about ways of providing helpful reactions to students' oral responses in class. To John Chapman, we say thank you for help in the early conceptualization of this work.

We are grateful to department chairpersons for searching out ways of better meeting the needs of students and for giving their faculty members support and encouragement to work with the integrated skills reinforcement approach. In particular, we would like to thank Roberta Matthews for reading early drafts of our materials and for providing advice on overall presentation; Ira Epstein, George Groman, John Hyland, and Herman Washington for ongoing support and especially for the leadership they exemplified by joining the ranks of trainees; and George Groman, too, for his work as this text's editor—his very thorough reading of our materials was much appreciated.

We owe thanks, also, to Kenneth Berger and LaGuardia's office of Institutional Research for helping us assess, each year, how far the project went and where it still had to go. We are indebted, too, to Nan Parmentier, Teachers College, Columbia University, for sharing with us her insightful analysis as an outside evaluator; we are sure that as a result of her work, the project has become immeasurably more successful in meeting students' needs.

We are extremely grateful to LaGuardia's administration, which is committed both to the "access model" of education and to a quality education for all its students. Our administration recognized that access and quality would require a new approach to teaching and over the past five years provided the support needed to develop and refine our program without assurances of success but with the belief that we would do our best. It was Martin Moed, our Vice President and Dean of Faculty, who saw the need and who articulated the challenge. From the start he listened and heard. He had faith in a budding idea and nurtured it, providing support in so many ways, and we are most grateful to him. To LaGuardia's President, Joseph Shenker, we are grateful as well for developing the kind of environment where people can work at their creative best. Our thanks also to Michael Hoban; without his encouragement we might never been able to get our student-centered faculty development model underway.

We owe thanks to others as well. To Dianne Bateman, Champlain Regional College, Montreal, we are grateful for critical analysis and thoughtful work. To Dean Carl Polowczyk and Jacqueline Stuchin and many of the faculty at Bronx Community College, we say thanks for believing in ISR and for piloting the training materials. To Gene Winter, Director of the Two-Year College Development Center, SUNY, Albany, and to Joseph Riley and CUNY's University-Faculty Senate's Committee on Remediation, we are most grateful for helping us share our materials and our model for faculty development with many interested, devoted teachers throughout our city and state. We also give special thanks to the Office of Academic Affairs and the Instructional Resource Center of the City University of New York for providing us with samples of student writing.

Since 1979 this project was, in part, made possible by funds from the New York State Education Department under the Vocational Education Act and the U.S. Office of Education under the Strengthening Developing Institutions Program, Title III. We thank them for their support. Without it we may never have been able to develop a model for training our own faculty, one which could be used by vocational and liberal arts faculties elsewhere. We owe particular thanks to Paul Chakonas, Jim Stratton, and Mike Van Ryn of the New York State Education Department (Voc Ed) for all of their consideration, care, and support over the years.

To Diane Loweth and Karen Bialkin, we wish to acknowledge a debt of gratitude—for their thoughtfulness, efficiency, and caring work in preparing the many editions of these materials.

To our editor, Tren Anderson, thanks for believing in and sponsoring a work with no models to fall back on.

Finally, to the many, many students who have used the ISR Learning Guides, thank you, on behalf of the faculty who created the guides and ourselves, for your honest reactions. We had, and still have, so much to learn from you.

Preface: A Student-Centered Approach to Faculty Development

This book was written by teachers for teachers. It grew out of what we think is an unusual faculty development program—a program rooted in concern for student learning, a program that began its work by asking: What problems do students experience in dealing with course content? How can we teachers help them overcome these difficulties?

The difficulties our students faced, however, were not unique to our college. The problems we saw existed and exist still in classrooms across the country, and declining SAT and ACT college entrance scores are but one indication that students are not coming to college as prepared as they used to be. More and more students are unable to deal comfortably with the substance of their courses.

Colleges as well as secondary institutions can address this problem in many ways: they can create comprehensive developmental skills programs with strictly enforced exit criteria to certify proficiency; they can create special programs for students for whom English is not a first language; they can set up peer-tutoring programs and learning centers; they can establish skills prerequisites, where appropriate, in all curricular areas. All this, however, may not be enough. Students entering with poor basic skills, even after they are brought up to acceptable levels, still may not have the same linguistic facility as students who enter college already possessing these skills. Then, too, the weaker students' skills are, the less faculty seem inclined to require students to use these skills—to read core works, to write extended papers, to make presentations, for example. So regression often occurs: students' newly emerging skills deteriorate as they move further away from developmental courses and into their subject areas. We sought, therefore, instructional approaches that would allow us to teach our subjects while simultaneously reinforcing students' use of language skills. For language, we knew, is not only an area of study but also, and perhaps more importantly, the tool for studying all other areas as well. As Georges Gusdorf once put it, "Man interposes a network of words between the world and himself, and thereby becomes master of the word."* By helping our students use their language skills in our courses, we were attempting to help them build such a network for mastering the disciplines as well as material beyond any one discipline or school.

Now, our faculty, like their colleagues in other colleges, had received no training in teaching in this way. In general their graduate study prepared them essentially for their field of inquiry, whether in a technical or

* *La Parole*. Trans. by Paul Brockelman. (Evanston, Ill.: Northwestern University Press, 1970), p. 7.

a liberal arts area. Even those who attended teachers colleges to learn instructional methods generally focused their work on traditional college students. For nowhere, to our knowledge, are people in subject areas systematically trained in the instructional techniques needed to teach effectively the students, "New Students" in K. Patricia Cross's terms, coming to college today. Not surprisingly, then, when a systematic training program evolved, our faculty responded enthusiastically to it.

Yet in the 1978–79 academic year, when LaGuardia Community College, a branch of the City University of New York, first set out to develop a language reinforcement program across its curriculum, it found that the task was much more complicated than anticipated.* First, the literature focused on the reasons *why* skills should be reinforced, not on specific techniques to help students make better use of their linguistic skills in exploring the disciplines. Further, what little had been done in the United States generally focused on only one of the skills areas, most often writing and occasionally reading. We found no programs that focused on integrating reading, writing, and oral/aural skills. Yet an integrated program seemed essential. When the British government, for example, set up a committee of inquiry to address and redress declining reading skills, it discovered that it could not do so by looking at reading alone. It found the expressive (speaking, writing) and receptive (listening, reading) modes of language critically interwoven. In fact, the title the committee selected for its final report, *A Language for Life*,† insists upon the ubiquitous role of language in our existence. Therefore, when the committee made its final recommendations, it called not for a national policy on reading but for a policy of "language across the curriculum."

Our program honored this recommendation. Initially, however, we sought to realize this policy for our institution alone. That is, LaGuardia Community College designed an approach for reinforcing language across the curriculum and in part through grant funds (from both the New York State Education Department under the Vocational Education Act and the U.S. Office of Education under the Strengthening Developing Institutions Program, Title III) developed, tested, and applied the strategies appearing in the pages that follow.

Finding no linguistically integrated model to draw on, we turned to our own experiences. We began with the premise that each term each faculty member discovers a few new strategies for strengthening students' use of language skills in learning course content. Perhaps the

---

* Although our initial focus was on language skills, we knew that mathematical competency and mastery of a wide range of subject areas called for constant application and reinforcement of math skills. Our thought was to pursue a language reinforcement program first, since the interrelationship of these skills seemed obvious, and then, once we had a model established, to pursue the math reinforcement. We are currently developing strategies for guiding students to apply math skills to the math-related content of various disciplines.

† Department of Education and Science, *A Language for Life*. Bullock Report. (London, England: Her Majesty's Stationery Office, 1975).

teacher begins the course by previewing with students the overall structure of the text, pointing out that subheadings provide a running outline of the material covered. Perhaps the teacher gives students sets of questions to guide reading or to focus listening or breaks down writing and oral assignments into their component parts to encourage success along the way. Such good approaches to integrating language into the curriculum existed in classrooms at our school and at other schools as well. Whatever strategy any one teacher created, chances were that some colleague in another area or even at another institution had already discovered that same strategy or might discover it shortly. Yet such "reinvention of the wheel" seemed a waste of valuable time.

Gradually, then, we realized the need to catalogue proven strategies, from which faculty could choose those that suit their students' needs while simultaneously adding to the pool of strategies for others to use. This text represents the beginning of such a pool of strategies. Teachers in liberal arts and technical areas have used the strategies in this book and have found them effective. Counseling and cooperative education staff also have found many of these strategies helpful in developing materials for academic advisement and for career-related seminars.

As you leaf through the text, you undoubtedly will find yourself reviewing some strategies and saying, "I do this." Indeed, we assumed that all good teachers would recognize at least one of these strategies in their everyday repertoire. In fact, while some of the strategies laid down in the pages that follow are new, others have been in general use in teaching for years. What we think is unique about their appearance here, however, is both their step-by-step presentation and their inclusion within a system of strategies for reinforcing language skills. The step-by-step approach is intended to guide readers as they apply the strategies to their own courses. The inclusion of strategies from the various linguistic modes is intended to help those teachers who wish to apply "language across the curriculum" to an entire course. This latter method we have come to call ISR: Integrated Skills Reinforcement—a holistic approach for helping students use all the modes of language for exploring and mastering course content.

What do teachers who have used the strategies say about them? They say that they sense a greater assurance and direction in their training. They note improved class performance in areas previously viewed as too difficult for students to master. Also, participating faculty have found a carryover of the strategies from a selected course both to other courses and to other professional activities. Instructors say that they internalize the integrated skills approach and cannot help but apply it to other dimensions of their work. "Once you start, there's no stopping. You wonder, 'How could I have taught any other way?' You just naturally use the method in your other courses."

All this is not to suggest that the integrated skills reinforcement approach does not demand a good deal from teachers. And we teachers already have a great many demands made on us. Gerald Hugh's parody is apropos: "*Monday*. Arriving at school in a decisive mood, I wrote on my 'Things to do' pad: (1) See the caretaker about the funny sticky stuff behind the radiator in room 3. (2) Remove the outdated notices from the board in the corridor. (3) Institute a language policy across the curriculum."*

It is, indeed, a formidable task to teach any subject, be it philosophy, accounting, painting, data processing, or psychology, without having to do any more. Yet the premise of the ISR approach is that language is not an appendage to the corpus of knowledge, but is its very heart. In truth, faculty at our school had initially feared that they would lose too much time focusing on language skills. However, as one participant put it, "I anticipated lost classroom time by implementing the strategies, but after the first few weeks, I found I actually gained time because students were better prepared."

This collection of strategies, of course, is not exhaustive. It is only a beginning. We trust that as you work with this book, you will be identifying additional strategies that you use both to reinforce language skills and to facilitate learning of content. We hope this text will become part of an ongoing discussion among faculty at different institutions on successful ways of teaching and reaching students. We hope our efforts stimulate the sharing of what is working behind closed doors.

JoAnn Romeo Anderson
Director, ISR Project

* *London Times Educational Supplement*, March 26, 1976.

A Guide for Using This Text

This text is divided into five major parts. The first part, "Strategies for Assessing Students' Communication Skills in Relation to Content Courses," enables you to assess students' abilities to use their reading, writing, oral, and listening skills to deal with your course's content. The next three parts—"Strategies for Helping Students Write for Content Courses," "Strategies for Encouraging Students' Effective Use of Oral and Listening Skills in Content Courses," and "Strategies for Helping Students Read Successfully in Content Courses"—outline methods for facilitating students' use of various modes of language in exploring and mastering course content. The fifth part, "Integrating Language Skills for Content Mastery," reflects the assumption underlying the text: language is an organic system whose receptive (reading, listening) and expressive (writing, speaking) modes are interdependent, together forming a system for learning. Hence the fifth part of the text describes how to put together for your course an ISR Learning Guide containing materials reflecting all the strategies presented in this text. To give you a sense of how the different strategies can work together to foster learning in a particular course, we have included a complete learning guide developed for a course in statistics. We have also included selections from guides in a range of courses (finance, literature, occupational therapy, linguistics, and others).

But why "strategy"? What we lay out on the following pages are more than techniques. They are practical plans for meeting particular problems. Each strategy begins with an overview of the issues to be addressed and then, in a step-by-step progression, offers a guide to applying the strategy to a course that you choose. Let us say, for example, that you wish to know whether students have the requisite skills needed to read your assigned text. The fourth strategy will walk you through the steps involved in gauging *your own* students' reading skills in relation to *your* required readings. If you should discover a discrepancy between your students' reading skills and the level of your assigned readings, other strategies will help (see Strategy 12,"Previewing Readings," Strategy 13, "Preparing Reading Guides," and Strategy 14, "Introducing Difficult Vocabulary"). One way to use this text, then, is to address a particular problem area—reading, perhaps, or listening, let us say—to choose the appropriate assessment strategy for that problem and then to select other strategies to help students manage course material.

Another way to use the strategies in this text involves an integrated skills reinforcement approach, an approach that builds all the strategies for reinforcing reading, writing, oral, and listening skills into your course. This approach takes time in preparing but in the long run pays off in students' preparedness and ability to deal more intelligently with the subject.

If you decide that you want to take this integrated approach, here is how those who have done it have found it helpful to proceed: (1) Choose a course that you think would benefit from language reinforcement. Be sure that the course is one that you enjoy teaching, for this will make the development of reinforcement materials enjoyable and will put you at your creative best. Be sure, also, that the course you choose is one that you will not be teaching for a term or so. This will give you the freedom to create at your own rate without pressure. (2) Select as the initial focus of your work the first unit of this course, and for this unit create the materials (for example, skills assessment materials, reading guide questions, questions to foster active listening and to promote focused discussion, writing tasks, and so on) that you need to apply all the strategies included in this text. (If the first unit is not really representative of other units, you may need to focus your initial work on the first two units of your course.) Teachers have found it critical to limit their early work to a unit or two in order to experience firsthand what integrated skills reinforcement means. Materials developed for the first or second unit (hereafter referred to as the "target" unit or units) then can serve as a model for the materials you develop for other units of the course. Assessment strategies, of course, and perhaps also the strategies for building longer writing and oral assignments into your course may be used only once; all other strategies, however, will most likely be applicable to every unit. (3) Once you have created materials applying all the strategies to your "target" unit, create materials applying the strategies to other units in your course. (4) Next, review the materials (e.g., course description, objectives, syllabus, and so on) that you presently give students, and then (5) create an ISR Learning Guide, which incorporates your usual materials and the ones you have just created for integrating language reinforcement across your course content. (See Part V of this text for a more detailed description of how to put together such a learning guide and for sample materials that you can use as references.)

The "integrated skills reinforcement" approach, however, need not be used solely for self-paced instructional development. It can be used successfully in a programmatic way as an instructional component of a faculty development program. Indeed, as Nelson and Siegel have shown, instructional development projects seem most successful when they focus on specific, usable skills and occur in group settings (see, for reference, *Effective Approaches to Faculty Development*, Washington, D.C.: Association of American Colleges, 1980). Below, for your reference, is a sketch of how ISR has been and can be used programmatically. Obviously, the particular needs of your institution, your colleagues, and your students may suggest modifications in the structure of such a program. However, an outline of a program that has proved viable elsewhere may suggest some starting points.

During the spring of the year preceding the implementation of the program, a core of faculty is selected to work with the program. We have found twenty to be a workable number. We also have found it useful to select faculty from a wide range of disciplines, including the skills areas, for even here faculty generally are not trained in an "integrated" approach to language. These faculty are given the text of instructional strategies, asked to review it, and asked to select as the focus of their work a course they enjoy teaching but one which they will not have to teach until the following spring. Then, during the opening sessions of the new academic year, participants are formally introduced to the concept of integrated skills reinforcement and to the program's format. Next, the twenty faculty members are divided into four groups, each having a team leader experienced in these methods. These groups function as independent teams throughout the year, meeting together weekly for approximately two hours.

Throughout the fall term, faculty study and examine the strategies in the text and devise their own classroom applications for a single unit in the selected course. Next, with the experience of the target unit as a base, each faculty member develops the materials needed to infuse linguistic strategies into the rest of the course. By the end of the fall term, then, participants have developed materials needed to apply all the strategies to their spring course. Faculty draw these materials into a learning guide, which is reproduced for each student's use.

During the spring term, each faculty member uses the learning guide in class and has an opportunity to videotape lessons. Videotaping has been found to be integral to the project because it provides teachers with a concrete frame of reference for informal review and assessment of skills reinforcement in the classroom, particularly the reinforcement of oral skills. An observer, of course, could provide such assessment, and in many instances, group members visit each other's classes and team leaders are invited to provide feedback. However, we have found it is important to use evaluation as a tool, not as a goal of the project. The basic goal is to help teachers to acquire and to develop facility with new reinforcement strategies so that students can better grasp subject matter. While outside assessment is valuable for assessing the project and for suggesting ways of improving its effectiveness, it should not be used to evaluate teachers. Such evaluation would undermine the very nature of a program which people participate in voluntarily. It is interesting to note that having an opportunity to see one's self on tape often reveals a very different picture from what one thought happened in the classroom. "I could have sworn I focused my questions more clearly," said one participant. "I was surprised that I didn't!" Of course, it should be clear that no one need see the tape except individual teachers themselves. However, many teachers do solicit responses from their team leaders or from group members. Some groups have even found it helpful to use the taped lessons as a basis for group discussion of how strategies transcend disciplinary boundaries. Indeed, this is a critical observation and one that strongly suggests the value of creating interdisciplinary work groups.

Throughout the spring term, faculty participants annotate their own materials as they teach from them, keep a running record of what works and what does not, and meet regularly with their group to discuss findings. At the end of the term, they make any needed modifications in their learning guides. By the beginning of the following year, each instructor has a guide tested for success in meeting student needs, a guide that can often serve as a valuable resource for other faculty, particularly adjunct faculty, who will be teaching the same course.

To be sure, we are not unaware of the promises made by teacher training programs. Many such programs focus on broad areas of instruction, leading discussions, let us say, without breaking them down into component parts. The result is that teachers know that they should introduce more discussion into their classes but may never become fully aware of all the subskills needed to use discussion most successfully. Our program breaks down into component parts instructional strategies for reinforcing language skills across the disciplines. Further, it provides an opportunity for faculty to develop individual materials for their own subject areas. Thus a select group is not off somewhere writing materials designed for others to use but eventually doomed, in fact, for a corner of a dusty shelf. With this program each faculty member develops materials for his or her own courses, builds into the materials personal teaching style, tests new approaches in the classroom, monitors the new experience through videotaping, and revises materials for future use.

Thus, as you see, you can use this book in many different ways. You can select an individual strategy or two to meet a particular need in your class. You can use the book to help you develop materials for an entire course, "integrated skills reinforcement" materials for helping students use all the modes of language for exploring and mastering course content. Or you can use it in a programmatic way; that is, to form an instructional development component of a faculty development program.

No one knows *the* right way to help students make more effective use of their language skills in learning course content. However, we believe our integrated and systematic approach has us moving in the right direction.

Integrated Skills Reinforcement

Part I

Strategies for Assessing Students' Communications Skills in Relation to Content Courses

1 | Gauging Writing Skills

Overview

When it comes to a page of prose, most of us are judges by second nature. As we read a journal article, a newspaper editorial, a letter from a business correspondent, a bank application, a tax form, something inside us says: "This is clear; I understand this. This is good." or "What is this thing trying to say? I just can't follow it; it doesn't make any sense." Instinctively we acknowledge and appreciate clarity, precision, and logic in writing as in other forms of communication; and we recognize and suffer frustration from prose that shows fuzzy thinking, that lacks focus or correctness or structure.

We bring our talents for judgment to student writing too. When we rate papers, it does not matter that we might fail to identify specific errors or that we feel inept about making appropriate comments about diction and style at the end of a research paper or of a midterm essay. We do, however, listen to the inner voice that says, "This student knows what she's talking about." or "This student has problems writing." In fact, that last familiar refrain is a song of assessment, and with it we are making judgments about literacy in our discipline. When we put grades on written work, we give them as judgments of content certainly, but we may also give them to reflect, at least to some degree, whatever instinct we have about good or bad writing.

Unfortunately, in many cases our basis for judgment is just that—instinct. It is easy to suppress that instinct, surely, by avoiding written work in a subject area, but that approach removes a vital rung in the student's climb to knowledge. Writing, after all, is not only a way of showing command of content but is also a means for acquiring it. In most courses students do write at least some of the time, and teachers do evaluate what they read on students' papers. Because we are busy, we may not formulate a reliable system for assessing student writing at the beginning of the term. However, if we take the time to do so, we will be in a better position to assist students to learn content by means of writing about it. Such a system ought to take into account a writer's abilities at the outset of the course, the goals for writing proficiency set by the institution for a given curriculum or career plan, the kinds of writing courses required of students, and the writing prerequisites for the course you teach.

Obviously, the men and women in your classes may have wide-ranging abilities as writers. Some may be beginners, taking formal instruction with a teacher of writing for the first time, yet they may show promise as writers. Others, despite years of training, may show little control over the written word. Still others may be considerably advanced in their composing skills. This mixed audience will be especially evident to you if your department requires no writing courses of students prior to admission into your course—a distinct possibility, unfortunately, at many institutions.

Discovering early in a course your students' general level of writing competency has great value both as you create writing tasks and as you think about individual students' development as writers. The steps in the following strategy are designed to help you, at the start of the course, gain a sense of where students stand in regard to their peers. The first step will help you identify the writing prerequisites for your course. The next step will guide you to consider samples of student writing so that you sharpen your sense of the range of prose students *will produce*, given admissions criteria at your college and the exit criteria from the various required writing courses there. The next will have you look at how well students in your sections can in fact write. A final step will suggest ways to arrange for extra help for students who need it. These steps lead to essential information: the relationship between students' abilities as writers and the kinds of writing tasks your course demands.

Strategy 1: Gauging Writing Skills

Step 1: Identify writing prerequisites. From the course description in the college catalogue or from the formal course proposal and statement of objectives approved by the institution, identify the writing courses required for students who take your course and the skills they should master when they complete the prerequisites.

Consider, for example, the following sample catalogue description:

HUA200 Art of the 20th Century
3 hours; 3 credits

This course explores the history of various styles and forms of Western art from the impressionist period to the present. Such diverse styles of Modern Art as Cubism, Dada and Surrealism, Expressionism, and the more recent styles of Pop and Conceptual Art will be discussed and explained. Consideration will be given to the understanding of abstract and nonobjective art as

> well as the influences which African
> and Eastern art forms have had on the
> development of modern art styles.
> Illustrated with slides and reproduc-
> tions. Museum visits required.
> Prerequisite: CSE099, ENG099

This art course at one community college demands two prerequisites, one of which is a basic reading course (CSE099), the other of which (ENG099) is a writing course. Checking in the college catalogue, you would discover that ENG099 is *Basic Writing*, a course coming before the freshman composition course in sequence. Scores on college place- ment tests in this institution determine which course a student will enter in the writing program, and a high enough score will mean that a student would skip English 099. Thus, depending on your school and the prerequisites it has established for college courses, you can expect students' writing abilities for your course to vary. Some of your students might be taking basic writing concurrently with your course; others might be required to take that basic writing course but might not yet have enrolled for it; others might be taking the required freshman com- position course; and still others, depending upon the level of your course, might have completed the required composition sequence a year or more ago with no formal writing instruction since then.

The point in all this is that although it is impossible even in the best of all academic worlds to determine with accuracy a common level of writing mastery for students in your class, looking at prerequisites allows you to see what demands the institution makes on the student as a writer. Those demands, ultimately, help you to establish writing assignments in your course.

Step 2: Become familiar with proficiency levels. Knowing prerequisites is only the first step in assessing students' writing early in the course. You have to know the kind of writing to expect after a student fulfills the particular prerequisites. Proficiency levels often vary from institu- tion to institution and from course to course, but a strong writing pro- gram will announce its exit criteria for required courses and will provide samples of student writing that meet those criteria. Additionally, some large state or city systems require all their students to take the same proficiency test, and these tests sometimes serve as standards either for entry into different composition courses or for passing courses at differ- ent levels.

For purposes of illustrating student writing at different levels, let us look at some samples from the writing skills assessment test that is part of the Freshman Skills Assessment Program (FSAP) of the City Uni- versity of New York. A student required to enroll in basic writing—

remedial or developmental are other terms used to describe this course preceding freshman composition—would write a sample such as this:*

(1) Recently I have watched some of television's top rate shows. (2) The shows have no educational value at all. (3) The violence and sex that the networks put out is outrageous. (4) Not only that, but it has an overall bad effect on grades in school. (5) The time these shows are air, interfers with time for study, term projects book reports, and homework.

(6) I do however; disagree that everyone should pull the plug on television. (7) Television does have its' positive side. (8) With the PBS (CHANNEL 13) education shows (NOVA, etc.). (9) Television is an excellent means of communication. (10) Television news has more information plus films so you have a feeling of what's happening and so you would be a bore.

(11) A solution is to allow maybe one hours of air time for network show an evening on weekdays and unlimited air time for weekends and holidays.

(12) The television could if used properly new tool of education if it is used wisely and by programming more educational series.

(13) Television is also a great advance. (14) It's a good feeling to come home and watch a show to relax you after a long days work.

This student needs to take a basic skills course for several reasons, although there are some strengths in her writing. The writer does show some ability to organize her ideas in the first four paragraphs. She uses connecting words at the beginning of paragraphs to suggest that her argument is logical (sentences 6 and 11). In addition, the essay has some good sentences, at least in the first half, and the writer has tried to use a vocabulary appropriate to her topic.

The essay, however, does not begin with a clear statement of the writer's position. Its development of ideas is weak because the logic of paragraphs one and two does not lead to the conclusion drawn in paragraph three. The third and fourth paragraphs are each only one sentence

---

* The assignment that led to this sample and to the other student samples in this section is reproduced below:

> It always strikes me as a terrible shame to see young people spending so much of their time staring at television. If we could unplug all the TV sets in America, our children would grow up to be healthier, better educated, and more independent human beings.
>
> Do you agree or disagree? Explain and illustrate your answer from your own experience, your observation of others, or your reading.

Both essays and commentary (which have been adapted here) appear in *The CUNY Writing Skills Assessment Test: Student Essays Evaluated and Annotated by the CUNY Task Force on Writing* (New York: Office of Academic Affairs, CUNY, 1980).

long, leaving their basic ideas undeveloped. The fourth paragraph is a better summary of the writer's position than the last paragraph, which goes off the subject and offers more arguments in favor of watching television. Then, too, the paper has problems in grammar and mechanics: sentence structure is wobbly toward the end particularly, and there are many misspellings and misuses of punctuation.

The student who wrote the paper below also would require a basic (remedial) course in writing, even though this paper shows more of a command over skills than the paper above:

(1) I disagree with the statement that television has a harmful effect on young people. (2) If we unplug all the TV set, it may result in an opposite way rather than it said in the passage. (3) This result maybe that children become ignorant and blind to the modern society. (4) Another words, they will not know what is going on in this world by means of news cast on television.

(5) However, it's undeniable to say television also has a harmful effect to the children because of some series shown on TV that deal with actions and violences. (6) But besides those series, there are programs that are shown to provide the young people the necessary knowledge and education. (7) These programs are often seen on channel thirteen which is considered an educational broadcasting company. (8) Many programs shown on which are excellent and interesting, and providing real and scientific knowledges to the viewers, such as NOVA, VISA and many others. (9) I have been watching these programs many times, although not becoming omniscient, I now understand more, so do the other people, the gradual advancement and improvement of this world.

(10) It is not necessary to have this kind of programs only on this public TV company. (11) Good programs can also be seen on those commercial TV broadcasting companies too. (12) There are certain hours that those channels will present some special series that are good to be watched. (13) For example, there are programs like "The Last of the Wild," "In Search of ...," etc. shown on these channels.

(14) Again, it is not necessary to watch just these excellent series. (15) There are news broadcasting on most of the channels too, and which gives the viewers the events of the world. (16) A television is good for those who are illiterary but able to listen and for those who are lazy enough to pick up a copy of a newspaper.

(17) It is true that children in recent years have imitated the characters on the TV shows and done the things these characters did. (18) Sometimes crimes are resulted. (19) It is also true that children become lazier on their homework but spend their times on TV. (20) Besides these weakness that the TV provides, remember, there are good programs described above. (21) There is only one way to

stop the belief of harmful effect of television, which is to find a way to halt those violent shows on TV and concentrate on those more educational programs.

This writer makes a point, sticks to it, and offers some specific details to support her views. She is able to introduce a number of different aspects of her subject and to keep them in reasonably clear relation to one another. The writer establishes useful paragraph divisions (with the exception of the misplaced sentence 5), and in her final paragraph, she points out opposing points of view (sentences 17–19).

This essay has problems, however, because the details the writer introduces are unexpanded and therefore unexplained (sentences 8, 13, and 15). As a result, although the writer has many potentially interesting ideas, they are not well developed. In addition, the writer's control of language and sentence structure is inconsistent. Her sentences are often tangles because of incorrect verb forms or lack of punctuation (sentences 8, 9, and 18). She confuses singular and plural forms (sentences 2, 3, 4, 8, 10, and 20) and misuses or omits articles (sentences 3, 6, and 16). Although the writer has a generally adequate vocabulary, she frequently puts words together incoherently and in that way confuses the reader. For example, "it may result in an opposite way" (sentence 2) and "there are news broadcasting" (sentence 15).

A student who completes a basic skills program in writing at CUNY—or a student for whom such a course may be waived—should be able to write clear paragraphs that show some control over content, although many errors might appear. (Remember that these students may not yet have taken the required freshman composition course at one of the units at the university.) On the basis of a paper such as the one below, a student would not be required to take basic skills instruction in writing.

(1) Television has a harmful effect on young people. (2) If a child is watching television he cannot explore the outside world for himself. (3) The violence on these shows could make him believe there is no good only bad and television takes away the child's ability to imagine, think or play.

(4) If a child is in the habit of watching television he cannot use his sense of curiosity to learn about things around him. (5) The television does this for him, he does not initiate this feeling on his own. (6) It might be good for a child to see a flower, for example, on t.v. but nothing can show how it really is, to take it in your own hands and describe it for yourself. (7) This is what t.v. is taking away from today's children. (8) Their sense to learn and to explore on their own. (9) These young people are depending on t.v. for something which they have already, but just do not use.

(10) Most of what is shown on television today is violence. (11) Since young people are watching so much t.v. violence could be the only thing that appeals to them and they carry this distruction to their own every day lives. (12) Children watching violence to much could get used to it, not care about real murders or wouldn't think a second time about picking a gun and killing somebody because his hero "Kojak" constantly does it on t.v. and he wants to be just like him. (13) Young children might not know the difference between the good guy or bad ones and sometimes on t.v. the bad guys are the heros the roles have changed considerably.

(14) Television takes away the child's ability to imagine, play and think for himself. (15) If a child is constantly watch t.v. he doesn't have time to imagine or play or think for himself. (16) Playing is good for a young child because he learns how to share and understand others by the use of toys. (17) By thinking a child can determine his values not use his favorite t.v. characters' values which might be invalid ones. (18) Imagining is taken away from the child because of t.v. advancement children can now go off to those far of lands that they used to imagine.

(19) Television has a distructive effect on a child. (20) He becomes addicted to it and does not go, outside to explore. (21) The child can take on invalid values seen on t.v. like violence. (22) T.V. can take away the ability for the child to use his own mind in everyday life.

The essay has a clear pattern of organization. The writer follows a simple five-paragraph form. She states her position and gives three reasons to support it in the first paragraph. She develops each reason in the next three paragraphs. And she concludes by restating the introduction. Each paragraph holds together pretty well. Specific illustrations help develop the argument in the middle paragraphs. The meaning of most sentences is clear, and the sentences are varied enough in length and structure to keep the reader interested. The writer's vocabulary seems adequate to her needs.

Despite these strengths, however, the writer does not connect ideas from paragraph to paragraph. This lack of transition weakens the overall logic of the essay. In addition, sentence beginnings and endings are sometimes not clear (sentences 5, 6, 8, and 18). The writer tries to put two or three ideas into the same sentence without sufficient skill in handling sentence structure to allow her to do something meaningfully (sentences 13, 14, and 18). Occasionally the writer uses language imprecisely (sentence 21) and is repetitious (sentences 15 and 16). She also misspells some common words.

As illustrations, the essays you have just examined give you a sense of the possible range of capabilities of writers in your class. Of course, each institution sets its own criteria, and by checking with departments that offer the courses, you will have to find out their expectations of students at different levels of progress through a writing program.

Step 3: Assign and collect brief writing samples. Even with a sense of the range of possible writing competencies in your class, you are right to acknowledge that there can be no exact correspondences between expectations and what writers actually produce. For example, although students may leave a basic skills course with a passing grade, they may have taken the course more than a year before taking yours, and even as sophomores or juniors, they may not yet have begun freshman composition. Therefore, a check of prerequisites alone rarely provides enough information for assessment. You may want also to devise a brief, easy writing task *for the first week of class*, a task whose product you can assess quickly. (One place to ask for this brief writing sample is on a skills questionnaire: see Strategy 15.) You are not going to grade this writing sample, remember; you want to read students' work just to get a sense of how people in the class write. On any personal information forms you require students to fill out, you can ask at least one question that demands a few full sentences in response. Or you may wish to make an early assignment rooted more in the content of your course. You might want to use one of these suggestions:

> On the paper I am handing out, write a few complete sentences introducing yourself to me. Tell me your name, where you went to high school, what you think the next two years in college hold in store for you.

> (or)

> This is a course called "Introduction to Social Science." Write three or four sentences telling what you expect to learn in a course such as this.

> (or)

> This is a course in mathematics. Most of you have taken some math before. On the paper I am now distributing, write a paragraph or two telling what you think mathematics is and how you felt about studying it in previous years.

> (or)

> Before we begin today, look over your class notes from yesterday and take fifteen minutes to write a summary of the main points of my lecture.

Step 4: Arrange for special assistance. As you review early writing in your class, you are bound to notice that some students have skills insufficient for quality performance in your course. Although you as the instructor will attempt to help individual students, clearly you cannot deal extensively with their skills as writers as you focus on your subject in class. However, your institution may offer a variety of support services for students. Perhaps the division of counseling or of academic affairs or perhaps the library or the media center offers special tutoring for anyone needing assistance for a course. Or perhaps your college has a writing center where students can receive help on a paper. If so, you

Writing Center Referral

Student _____

Course _____

Please provide assistance in the following areas:

1._____

2._____

3._____

4._____

_____
Instructor's Signature

Figure 1.1

should suggest that students with problems as writers attend regularly. Make the suggestion directly on the page produced by the student, and highlight the problem requiring attention. If the writing center issues a referral form, use it to simplify procedures. Or you can make up your own referral form. A sample appears in Figure 1.1.

These techniques for assessing writers early in the term and for providing any required extra help should go a long way in helping you establish realistic writing activities for your class.

2 | Gauging Oral Communication Skills

Overview

Students, being human, talk a great deal. They talk to friends, parents, brothers, sisters, storekeepers, salespeople, teachers, lovers, strangers. They talk to dogs, perhaps plants, themselves. They talk in person, over the phone, on tape machines. For speech is the most human activity, indeed *the* distinguishing human activity, one we begin to learn unconsciously, effortlessly it seems, before we even learn to walk. It is tempting, therefore, to take this most natural and human of enterprises for granted. As teachers, we may express concern over our students' writing but may find ourselves passing over oral communication. We assume, perhaps, that the oral area, unlike the written area, is a "natural" one. After all, we have been at it since the cradle.

There is, however, a vast difference between speaking and speaking effectively. Effective speaking, like effective writing, is a skill requiring careful instruction and guidance. Yet it is only recently that governmental agencies, professional organizations, and, for that matter, educational institutions have begun to see oral communication as one of the basic skills. It is only recently that the talk about a crisis in literacy has begun to touch on the relationship between speaking and the other communication skills—reading and writing.

While some awareness of this critical area of oral skills is growing, few high school or college programs attempt to help students *systematically* develop the oral communication skills they need for educational and professional success. To be sure, some institutions have sought to escape the rigidity of the classical systems of rhetoric and to create a more "relevant" curriculum. They have tended to abandon the more traditional public speaking courses in favor of courses focusing on the more informal and more common interactions in which people communicate interpersonally or in groups. However, such courses are generally not required, and so students' oral communication skills most often go unattended both in high school and in college much as they have in primary school.

Yet students themselves generally recognize the need to develop competencies in speaking. For example, college graduates have been found to rank oral skills as among those most needed after graduation but among those receiving the least attention in college. Similarly, students still attending college reveal that they perceive their academic programs as offering insufficient instruction in oral and interpersonal skills. Then, too, many students express fear of speaking in spite of an awareness that the need for speaking well will be a pressing demand after graduation.

Such fears of course, are not groundless. Employers of today's graduates, in field after field, seek employees with strong skills in oral communication. Employers often cite an applicant's inability to communicate as the reason for rejection and an applicant's ability to communicate effectively as an important consideration in hiring.

As teachers, we know that students need communication skills not only for success in their future professions but also for success in their courses. We have all seen students advance their understanding through classroom discussion, pointed questions and answers, and thoughtful summaries. Similarly, we all have watched students with poor communication skills flounder in class discussion. Though different teachers, no doubt, have faced different problems, we have all seen at one time or another students who were unable to marshal details to support a generalization or who were unable to generalize from specific examples or who were unable to ask questions that might lead them from confusion. In addition, we have seen students whose grammar, pronunciation, or constant use of "I mean" has left us and our classes wondering just what they *did* mean. There seems to be a growing presence of such problems in the surface, or "form," areas of our students' speech (*how* we say what we say) as well as in the deeper "content" areas (*what* we in fact say).

Perhaps philosophers, psychologists, and linguists will one day resolve the ancient battle over language and thought—which precedes which, which needs which. Until then, however, what will remain certain is the critical interrelationship of the two. So whether or not we assume that higher-level thinking can exist without language, what is clear is that at some point we rely upon language to advance our thinking just as we rely upon language to convey our thoughts to others. Imagine a classroom, for example, in which teachers and students do not rely upon oral language to reach and to relate understandings. Having our students speak in class remains a certain way of both advancing and of assessing knowledge and understandings.

It is important, therefore, as teachers in the disciplines, to determine early in a course any problems that might inhibit students from talking through or sharing thoughts about course content. Clearly, as content teachers, we will not have the time to make a thorough examination of each student's oral skills. However, a brief investigation of the strengths and weaknesses of a particular class will help us design activities in ways that encourage students to build and draw upon skills needed for mastering the course curriculum.

The steps in the following strategy will help you judge just what speaking strengths and problems your students have. Such an assessment is worth the small investment of time, for ultimately the knowledge you gain will help you guide students through activities bringing significant rewards in learning.

Strategy 2: Gauging Oral Communication Skills

Step 1: Review some of the oral skills and problems that can come up in your classroom. Although what we say and how we say it are inexorably intertwined, it is helpful pedagogically to think of oral skills in two distinct categories: content-related skills (skills focusing on what is said) and form-related skills (skills focusing on how it is said).

When reflecting on your students' "content-related" oral skills, you will want to ask yourself, do your students

- Distinguish fact from opinion, or do they tend to offer opinions when the discussion requires facts and details?
- Offer their own understanding of material, or do they simply parrot what has been given to them?
- Draw generalizations from information and examples, or do they offer personalized examples when the discussion calls instead for broad conclusions?
- Stay on the subject, or do they distract listeners by shifting topics and by not answering the question?
- Provide responses that show a depth of understanding, or do they answer superficially?

When reflecting on "form-related" oral skills, you will want to ask yourself, do your students

- Use silent pauses while they think and talk through ideas, or do they make excessive use of distracting "verbal fillers" such as "like" and "you know"?
- Use their voices effectively, or do they speak too softly to be heard or to have credibility?
- Pronounce words correctly, or do they eliminate or add syllables or distort certain sounds?
- Use words correctly or do they use words inappropriately?
- Express ideas concisely, or do they ramble on and on?
- Have command over appropriate grammar and usage, or do they use nonstandard English in situations where standard English is expected?
- Present ideas logically, or do they express their ideas in ways that are difficult to follow?

Obviously, the lists of content- and form-related problems above are not exhaustive. You may come up with other skills and other problem areas to listen for when you make your assessment.

Step 2: Identify activities you can use to gauge your students' communication skills. Once you have reflected upon some of the communication skills and problem areas that seem to occur in your classroom, you will need to create an assessment activity or activities. One possibility is a brief informal assignment early in the course, an activity in which students speak to get acquainted with each other or with course material. For instance, in a career-oriented course, students might describe the genesis of their interest in their present work activities or even their future career plans. If well designed, such an introductory activity helps create a supportive learning environment while at the same time helping to provide the teacher with an opportunity to listen carefully to students' speech. Then, too, some teachers find that no single activity accurately gauges the wide range of oral communication skills demanded by their courses. However, it is still useful to attempt some assessment early in the course. It may make sense, then, to review your syllabus and to identify several representative activities, preferably ones occurring during the first two weeks of class, that will provide opportunities for you to gauge students' oral skills.

Step 3: Develop a means for keeping a record of skills requiring attention. It is easy to forget what you hear, and so you will want to develop some format for keeping track of potential problem areas as they come to your attention. Some easy and obvious methods include noting problems alongside students' names in your record book, writing down problem areas as they arise but only noting particular students' names when skills deficits seem to need serious attention, or preparing a sheet with common problems listed at the top for your own reference and then jotting down a particular student's name and checking off his or her particular difficulty as it comes to your attention.

Of course, you will need to be subtle when you take your notes. There are few things that produce more anxiety than to have the teacher writing feverishly while the student talks.

Step 4: Arrange for special assistance. As you review the notes you take over the first few weeks, you may notice students who have skills inadequate to make the most of your course. Adopting some of the strategies outlined in Part III of this book will help students speak more effectively in your course. You may also want to provide students with help individually. Clearly, you will not have time to dwell extensively on individual problems; you can, however, quickly identify areas in the school where specific students can get the additional assistance they may need. You may want to identify a liaison in the speech communication depart-

```
Student Referral:

Course Enrolled:

Date:

       I am referring this student to you for assistance in the
areas I have indicated.  We both would appreciate your help.

                              Sincerely,


                              _____


CONTENT-RELATED ORAL SKILLS:  what students say

[ ]   to give a fact or an opinion as requested

[ ]   to draw generalizations

[ ]   to give focused responses

[ ]   to provide in-depth analyses


FORM-RELATED ORAL SKILLS:  how students say what they say

[ ]   to use silent pauses (as opposed to verbal fillers
      such as "like" and "you know") appropriately

[ ]   to use voice effectively (volume)

[ ]   to pronounce words correctly

[ ]   to use words correctly

[ ]   to use appropriate grammar

[ ]   to organize ideas logically


OTHER COMMENTS
```

Figure 2.1

ment or in a skills lab. You can informally suggest to individual students that they meet with the liaison you identified, you can use the appropriate available referral form, or you can create a referral form for your own use and make clear to the receiving individual or department how and when you will use it. A sample form is given in Figure 2.1. If you find many students with oral communication problems, such a form will ultimately save you time. If, however, the student with a significant difficulty is rare, you may simply want to write a note introducing the student and his/her situation to an appropriate colleague or support center.

3 | Gauging Listening Skills

Overview

Even before we can see, as infants in the womb, we are listening—to steady rhythms and sudden sounds, all the time adjusting our movements to these unspoken messages that surround us. In the course of our lives, listening remains a dominant activity: it is estimated that we spend about half of our waking days taking in verbal messages. In terms of sheer volume alone, listening provides us with the bulk of information we receive in our lives. Listening, then, is a crucial component in human communication, the skill upon which many other skills build progressively. Without a good ability to listen, speech and reading and writing develop only with great effort. Indeed, it may be said that listening is the *basic* basic skill.

In our classrooms we rely upon our students' use of aural skills to absorb information and concepts presented in lectures and discussions. Even in the most student-centered classroom, students are asked to spend most of the time listening. Yet despite carefully constructed lectures and discussions, from students' tests, papers, and spoken responses it can often seem that students are not taking in what they need to take in. Of course, some students' undeveloped questions or vague answers may have us wondering whether these students are doing their reading and reviewing class notes. However, we can wonder, too, whether students are listening and listening well. Perhaps it is important details that we sense students are not "hearing," or the sequence of points in discussion, or the main point of the lesson. Our concern may vary from class to class, student to student, but as teachers even a single instance concerns us.

In a sense, it is not at all surprising that good listening is not as pervasive as we would like. For one thing, despite its acknowledged status as the "first" basic skill, listening is not really taught in our schools; hearing, like speaking, develops so naturally that it tends to be taken for granted. But hearing is not listening. Hearing is simply the physiological process of oral message reception. Listening, on the other hand, is a complicated process that transforms the received message into meaning.

The complex tasks involved in good listening also account for students' not listening as well as we would like. It is difficult to listen well. First, we have to focus our attention, deciding which sounds among countless sounds we will listen to, which voices among many voices, perhaps. We have to discard thoughts about the weather, about unpaid bills, about the new carburetor for the car; all these can distract us. Then, once we have focused on a discrete unit of communication, we have to determine just what the communication means—what it is about, how it is organized, how it is stated, whether it is valid, whether we already know it, whether we have use for the information, whether it is worth remembering. And all this is going on while the bells ring and planes fly overhead. No wonder, then, that the average listener, right after listening to someone speak, is said to remember only about half of what he or she has been told.

Careful listening requires work. As teachers responsible for imparting our disciplines to our students, we do not have time to teach the basic skill of listening. But since good listening in the classroom can mean the difference between students' confusion or enlightenment in regard to important subject matter, some attention to this skill is necessary. Early in your course you will want to know not only whether your students are imparting oral messages effectively but whether they are receiving them effectively as well. Are they listening to take in new points, or are they just filing new points away in old conceptual cubbyholes, reducing new knowledge to the old and familiar? Are they distinguishing between facts and inferences, or are they taking one for the other? Are they distinguishing major from minor points, or are they confusing these different levels of knowledge? Are they grasping the organization of the lesson, or are they blinded by the glare of related, though perhaps not significant, detail? Without a sense of how our students receive the critical information and concepts making up classroom messages, we cannot be certain that our most carefully planned lectures and discussions are getting through, nor can we make the necessary adjustments to assure that they do.

The steps in the following strategy will help you assess how well your students are listening to classroom communications. Listening and thinking may not be one and the same, but no one can deny that they are related. Listening is a critical process by which we make sense of what we hear. Assessing how well your students are listening will help you determine whether or not you have met your objectives in the classroom.

Strategy 3: Gauging Listening Skills

Step 1: Identify activities that provide opportunities for students to listen and for you to gauge their ability to listen. It is probably safe to say that students tend to function at a certain level of listening over the course of the term, though anything from the weather outside to the content of a specific lesson will affect students' motivation to listen on any given day. To assure that your assessment is not idiosyncratic, then, you will want first to identify two or three activities that occur early in your course (preferably during the first three weeks), activities that provide opportunities for students to listen and for you to gauge their general listening ability. These activities might include lectures, films, group discussions, and so on.

Step 2: Create a mechanism for gauging students' level of listening. Once you have identified two or three activities which require students to listen, you are ready to assess students' listening abilities. This is not an easy task, however. For listening, like reading, is an internal process, and to assess this process, you must ask students to externalize what it is they have heard and understood. This presents problems of measurement. If students speak or write in order for you to assess how well they listen, their ability to speak and/or write effectively will affect the message they transmit. If they express their understandings clearly and concisely, you can be assured they have listened well. If they do not express their understandings clearly, however, you may not be able to discern whether the problem is one of poor listening skills or an inability on the part of the student to express him- or herself in oral or written form. One practical way to avoid this dilemma is to develop a set of multiple-choice questions to test comprehension of specific segments of material.

You may decide, however, that the expression of ideas in more extended oral or written form is valid and consistent with course demands. In this case you may want to develop a few short-answer questions to assess listening. Or you may ask students to write a summary of the main points covered in class, setting aside a few minutes at the end of a few sessions to do so. Or you may find it interesting to gauge students' listening by using students' own recording of what they hear in class—i.e., by reviewing the notes students take in class. (To do this, you will want to bring carbon paper to class and to tell students that their task is to take good notes, which you will collect at the end of the session. You can say you are interested in seeing how well you are getting across and how well they are listening. Both will be true.) Some energetic teachers collect class notes regularly and work on an individual basis with students who have trouble grasping concepts or organizing what they have heard. If time allows, such an approach seems worthwhile, reinforcing in students the importance of careful listening and good note-taking and providing teachers with an ongoing sense of their students' performance in these critical areas.

Whatever means you use to assess students' listening skills, you will want the content of the target lessons to be tied in with the range of mental operations you expect students to perform as they listen to material throughout your course. For listening, of course, goes beyond physiological hearing to a point where it cannot be easily separated from such mental operations as recalling, summarizing, sorting, and evaluating.

Listening to or reading students' responses to questions you posed, as well as reviewing their notes, can be a real learning experience for you. You may be quite pleased and find that students have accurately grasped the material and accurately recorded what they learned for future study and review. You may, however, find students who remembered the examples but lost the main ideas, students who drowned in the details, or students who experienced difficulty organizing and recording what they learned. For such students, assistance of a practical sort is important.

Step 3: Arrange for special assistance. If as you review the results of these activities, you find students with skills inadequate to make the most of your course, you probably will want to look at Strategy 9 in this text in order to help your students listen more effectively. You may also want to help students individually. However, if for some students the problem seems to be a more serious one, you may want to identify a support service at your institution which can provide the attention needed. This may be found in any number of areas including the speech communication department, the reading department, the learning center, or even the student services department, where workshops on listening and other study skills are frequently offered.

4 | Gauging Reading Skills

Overview

Some people fear that the focus on media in American culture will mean the demise of reading. Television and movies bring immediate gratification, while books and other written materials often seem distant and demanding. Yet whether or not you believe there always will be a need for written language, for now, and indefinitely into the future, much vital information, as well as reflections on this information, exists in written form. Indeed, literacy remains the chief means of access to culture and knowledge.

But what about students who have difficulty reading? To be sure, all printed materials may not be a problem for them. Students read fiction, newspapers, magazines, and so on. Reading a textbook or a technical article, however, is quite a different matter, and often students do not have the specific skills needed to read these materials with sufficient comprehension to master the subject matter within them. As teachers we recognize the importance of students' reading, but to help them, we need to have some idea both of the reading skills our students possess and of the difficulty of our assigned reading in relation to students' skills. Only with this information in hand can we determine the extent to which students will be able, independently, to deal with our reading assignments and whether we will need to adopt additional strategies, such as those described in this book, in order to help students make more effective use of their reading skills in learning course content.

The following strategy will help you assess discrepancies between students' reading skills and the reading level of your assigned materials. Should such an assessment reveal less than adequate skills, you do not need to abandon or modify your course assignments in favor of fewer or less difficult readings. This approach can foster a further falling away of students' skills. Rather, an awareness of students' reading abilities will suggest ways to assist students as they study and read materials for your course. The steps you will need to follow to implement this strategy are outlined below.

Strategy 4: Gauging Reading Skills

Step 1: Determine the "reading grade level" of your students. There are many ways to get a general idea of students' reading grade level. If your school uses a placement test, you may be able to obtain the reading scores for each of your students as well as an analysis of what these scores mean. Also, if your school offers developmental reading courses, you can find out which of these courses are prerequisites for your course and at what level students leave the various reading classes. Your school catalogue may be helpful in determining such prerequisites. A sample course description follows. Note that the prerequisite listed is Basic Reading III, a course, upon reference, found to have an exit reading level of the eleventh grade.

Art 101
3 periods; 3 credits
Prerequisite: Basic Reading III or waiver

An exploration of a variety of art forms. Museum visits, studio experiences, and readings in aesthetics form the basis of the course.

Now to understand better what a reading level is, let us look at the following samples* designed to represent more or less the eighth, ninth, and eleventh grade levels. A student reading at the respective grade levels should be able to read the material without much difficulty.

Sample passage at approximately the eighth level:

You own an office. You buy ten typewriters for two thousand dollars. Five years later, the equipment is worth only five hundred dollars. Ten years later, the equipment is worth only one hundred· dollars. The equipment has decreased in value. This depreciation is true of almost all equipment. It is used. It gets older. It can not work as well as when it was new. Certainly it does not look new. As a result, the value of the equipment goes down.

In the above paragraph, the sentences are short and contain basic, easy-to-understand vocabulary. Also, only one concept, depreciation, is discussed.

Sample passage at approximately the ninth level:

A business buys a $200.00 typewriter and ten years later sells it for $50.00. What happened to the other $150.00? That money was deducted from the value of the typewriter because of wear and age. This decrease in value is called *depreciation.*

---

* Samples are taken from *The Reading Line Business* by Irene M. Reiter (New York: Cambridge Book Company, 1973), pages 21–23.

The typewriter is equipment. Such equipment is a *fixed asset*. Each year fixed assets decrease in value, and each year companies note that depreciation. Every year the typewriter in the example is worth $15.00 less than the year before.

In the second passage, the sentences are longer but the conceptual level is the same and the vocabulary is still quite basic.
Sample passage at approximately the eleventh level:

Almost every business has certain equipment, fixed assets, whose value depreciates as it gets older. Businesses compute the depreciation in a simple manner. They use the original cost of the equipment. Then they subtract the value they expect the equipment to be worth after a certain number of years. The difference between the original value and the expected value is the maximum amount of depreciation.

In this third passage, while the concepts again remain the same, sentences are still more complicated and vocabulary more sophisticated.
In order further to appreciate reading levels, consider a definition of depreciation from a "college-level" text (*Management Theory and Practice* by Ernest Dale, New York: McGraw-Hill, 1978, page 631). The vocabulary is much more difficult and includes new concepts such as *amortize* and *capital assets*.

Depreciation: Money set aside each year to amortize investment in capital assets whose value declines over time.

Note that the above "college-level" definition of depreciation is a good deal more difficult than the definitions offered by the three preceding samples. Then, too, most texts written on a college level will present many concepts at once, and these will be, in general, more conceptually sophisticated than *depreciation*. A greater number of concepts or more sophisticated ones will make material more difficult to read for some students.
After determining the approximate reading level of students enrolled in your course, you may want to turn your attention to the actual reading materials you assign to get a more accurate sense of how students will fare with your course reading.

Step 2: Determine the readability level of the materials you assign. Most publishers will provide you with the reading level of a text. However, if you are unable to obtain this information or if you want to determine the reading level of an article or monograph, you easily can do it yourself by using something called a readability formula. You should be aware, however, that helpful as readability formulas are, none provides a measure of conceptual difficulty; in general, a passage is more difficult than the reading level indicates. This will be discussed in more detail later on.

A particularly popular formula, one used by most publishers, is the Fry *Graph for Estimating Readability* (see Figure 4.1). The Fry graph gives the approximate "readability" based on *length of sentences and number of syllables.*

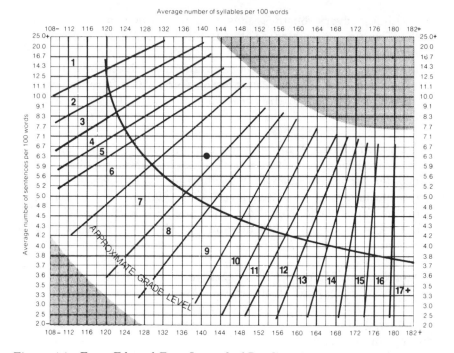

GRAPH FOR ESTIMATING READABILITY —EXTENDED

by Edward Fry, Rutgers University Reading Center, New Brunswick, N.J. 08904

Figure 4.1   From Edward Fry, *Journal of Reading, 21*(3), p. 249.

Following are the procedures for using the "Fry" should you need them.*

1. Randomly select three sample passages from a particular reading. Usually it is better to avoid specialized materials such as introductory sections or conclusions. Then, for each passage, count out the first 100 words and circle the 100th word. (A word is defined as a group of symbols with a space on either side; *thus, Joe, IRA, 1945, 8000,* and & are each one word. Do count proper nouns, initializations, and numerals.)
2. Count the number of syllables in each of the 100-word passages, and record the total for each. If you do not have a hand counter available, an easy way is to mark off each syllable by putting

---

* Instructions were adapted from those published by Edward Fry in *Journal of Reading, 21*(3), p. 249.

a slash after it. Then, when you get to the end of the passage, you can merely count the number of marks. (When counting syllables for numerals and initializations, count one syllable for each symbol. For example, *1945* is four syllables, *IRA* is three syllables, and & is one syllable.)

3. Determine the average number of syllables in the three passages and record it.
4. Count the number of sentences in each of the 100-word passages, estimating the length of the fraction of the last sentence to the nearest one-tenth. Record the total for each passage.
5. Determine the average number of sentences in the three passages and record it.
6. Enter the graph with average sentence length and the average number of syllables, and plot a point where the two lines intersect. This will give you the approximate grade level.

Note: If from paragraph to paragraph a great deal of variability is found in your syllable count or sentence count, putting more samples into the average is desirable.

Figure 4.2 is an example of this procedure that uses an art textbook. Note how the number of syllables and the number of sentences are marked off.

Although there continues to be some questioning of the method and its uses, the Fry readability formula is described here for several reasons. One is that it is a fast method for determining readability, and most experts agree that it correlates highly with the Dale-Chall (.94) and the Flesch (.96) readability formulas. This means that it is a good general indicator of reading level and can be of use for our purposes. (The Dale-Chall formula, for example, uses uncommon words and average sentence length to compute readability and takes much longer than the Fry.) The Fry also has the second advantage of giving the teacher a "hands-on" contact with the text in terms of words and sentence length. A third, but important, consideration is that the Fry formula is relatively easy to use.

The Fry readability formula, however, does not present a complete picture of readability in terms of technical vocabulary, concepts, and syntactical difficulty. Material that can seem very easy according to the Fry formula (short sentences made up of one- or two-syllable words) actually can be very difficult for students to comprehend if the material is highly technical (especially if it makes use of technical symbols) or highly theoretical or philosophical. For example, the sentence, "A man's reach should exceed his grasp," is a short sentence with primarily one-syllable words, yet it asserts an extremely sophisticated concept. Relying upon metaphor, the concept, though stated in simple language, would evade many weak readers. In fact, no readability formula will show fully the range of linguistic, syntactical, and conceptual difficulties that await student readers. As a result, we should always be aware of possible syn-

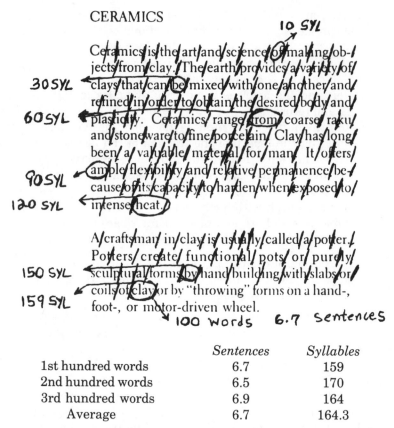

	Sentences	Syllables
1st hundred words	6.7	159
2nd hundred words	6.5	170
3rd hundred words	6.9	164
Average	6.7	164.3

Figure 4.2   Excerpt from page 103 in WE CREATE ART CREATES US, Brief Edition, by Duane Prebble. Copyright © 1976 by Harper & Row, Publishers, Inc. By permission of the Publisher.

tactical structures that may make our assigned readings difficult for our students. These include the use of the passive voice and the use of many qualifiers and modifiers.

Step 3: Determine discrepancies between reading levels of students and materials. You have now estimated the reading levels of both your students and your assigned reading materials. The next step is to determine any significant differences between the level of the required readings and the lowest possible reading level of students in your course. This information will be of use as you develop assignments.

Step 4: Create a Cloze test to assess further any discrepancies between students' reading grade levels and the reading level of your assignments. One way to get beyond the pitfalls of readability formulas is to assess your students' reading ability in relation to specific reading material by developing and administering something called a Cloze test. In this test, a sample 250-word passage is selected from a reading and presented to students with certain words deleted. (A sample appears in

Figure 4.3.) Students are asked to "fill in the blanks" by using their reading of the entire passage. A student's performance on this test will show you how well you can expect the student to handle assigned materials.

There are many applications of the Cloze test. It can be used to test for knowledge in a particular subject (by deleting key content words), or it can be used to determine reader ability to predict from print and to reconstruct an author's text. The third application, however, is what interests us here: using a Cloze test to assess a student's ability to comprehend a particular text. The advantage of the Cloze test is that you are not looking at only the student (reading "grade") or the text (readability "level") but at both, *at how the student interacts with your text*.

The following paragraph describes how to create and interpret a Cloze test based on your primary reading material and how to use the test results. It is important to remember that most students will be unfamiliar with Cloze test procedures and may find them difficult at first. Therefore, it is important to tell students that anxiety and at least some frustrations are to be expected. If you administer the Cloze test early in the term, you will be able to make a rapid assessment of students' skills and to prepare classes with this information in mind.

Select a *typical* 250-word passage from the body of your textbook. (As with the Fry, it is better to avoid specialized materials such as introductory sections or conclusions.) Then make a copy of the page or pages, and on the copy cross out every fifth word, but without including numbers or proper nouns among the words omitted. Have it retyped, substituting an underlined blank of ten spaces for the deleted "fifth" words. A sample is given in Figure 4.3. You may also wish to include, in their complete form, preceding and following paragraphs to give the section continuity. If this is not practical, at least leave the first sentence of the paragraph intact. Ask students to complete the passage by filling in the missing words, one word per blank. When scoring students' responses, accept appropriate synonyms and misspellings, since they will not detract from comprehension. The students' scores will indicate the level at which they can read the material—*independent, instructional*, or *frustrational*.

The following table shows the relationship between students' scores on a Cloze passage and the reading level at which you can expect them to function:

Percentage/Number Correct out of 50	*Level*
60% or more (30 or more answers correct)	Independent level
40% to 55% (20 to 28 answers correct)	Instructional level
40% and below (19 and below answers correct)	Frustrational level

Cloze Test

Monetary System of the United States

The essential role of a monetary system in the operation and development of financial institutions to supply credit to business, agriculture, consumers and the government was explained in Chapter 1. In this chapter, the nature and the functions of money are developed more fully, and the nature of the monetary system of the United States is also described and analyzed. Consideration is also given to the monetary standard on which the system is based and to the types of money currently in use to meet the needs of the economy.

Nature and Functions of Money

In the discussion of _____1_____ early development, money was _____2_____ as anything which is _____3_____ accepted as a means _____4_____ paying for goods and _____5_____ and of discharging debts. _____6_____ function of money is _____7_____ referred to as that _____8_____ serving as a medium _____9_____ exchange. This is the _____10_____ function of money in _____11_____ economy, but money also _____12_____ other functions. It serves _____13_____ a store of purchasing _____14_____ and as a standard _____15_____ value.

Money may be _____16_____ as a store of _____17_____ power which can be _____18_____ on at will. This _____19_____ be done shortly after _____20_____ is received or after _____21_____ has been held for _____22_____ period of time. While _____23_____ is held, it becomes _____24_____ liquid

Figure 4.3 From Ronald W. Melicher and Merle T. Welshans, *Finance: An Introduction to Financial Markets and Institutions* (Cincinnati, Ohio: Southwestern Publishing Co.), pp. 17–18.

asset for its _____25_____ and provides flexibility in

_____26_____ decision to spend or _____27_____ invest. But

the owner _____28_____ for this flexibility since _____29_____

is necessary to forego _____30_____ potential return that

could _____31_____ earned by investing the _____32_____ or

the satisfaction that _____33_____ be received from spending

_____34_____ for goods and services. _____35_____ can

perform its function _____36_____ a store of purchasing

_____37_____ only if its value _____38_____ relatively stable

or is _____39_____ .

The function of serving _____40_____ a store of purchas-

ing _____41_____ can also be performed _____42_____ an asset

other than _____43_____ if it can be _____44_____ into money

quickly and _____45_____ significant loss of value.

_____46_____ is the case with _____47_____ deposits held in

commercial _____48_____ and in mutual savings _____49_____

and with savings and _____50_____ shares and savings certifi-

cates. Such liquid assets reduce the need for holding money

itself as a store of purchasing power.

The third function of money--that of a standard of

value--refers to the fact that prices are expressed in terms of

the monetary unit and that contracts for deferred payments are

also expressed in this way. Prices and debts are usually

expressed in terms of dollars without any statement as to the

type of money to be used. The relationship of money as a stan-

dard by which to judge the value of goods is a circular one.

Figure 4.3 (continued)

The value of money may be stated in terms of the goods it will buy, and a change in the value of money. If money is to perform its function as a standard of value, it is essential that the value of the monetary unit be relatively stable.

Omitted Words

Paragraph One

1. its	6. this	11. any
2. defined	7. generally	12. serves
3. generally	8. of	13. as
4. of	9. of	14. power
5. services	10. basic	15. of

Paragraph Two

16. held	24. a	32. money
17. purchasing	25. owner	33. could
18. drawn	26. the	34. it
19. may	27. to	35. money
20. it	28. pays	36. as
21. it	29. it	37. power
22. a	30. the	38. is
23. money	31. be	39. increasing

Paragraph Three

40. as	44. converted	48. banks
41. power	45. without	49. banks
42. by	46. this	50. loan
43. money	47. time	

Figure 4.3 (continued)

The *independent* reading level is the one at which a student recognizes most of the words, comprehends well, and feels at ease while reading. At this level, the student needs no assistance in reading the material. At the *instructional* reading level, the student is not as familiar with vocabulary, has reduced comprehension, but with preparation and guidance by the instructor does not feel frustrated by the material. At the *frustrational* reading level, the student, even with assistance from the instructor, experiences considerable difficulty in his or her attempt to read and comprehend.

When you use a Cloze test to compare students' reading ability with material used in class, prepare students for the test by explaining the purpose and procedures of the test. Additionally, be sure to mention that the test will have no effect on their grades. Finally, the Cloze reading test should not be taken as the final word on students' ability or inability to comprehend material. Much will depend on the preparation for reading that students receive. Strategies 12, 13, and 14 may be useful here.

Besides creating a Cloze test and determining readability of your reading materials through the Fry formula, you may also wish to create your own informal tests to see whether your students are familiar with the vocabulary and concepts taught in your course. For example, you can create matching tests for key vocabulary words and concepts or a Cloze test procedure with key vocabulary words deleted (rather than every fifth word). Also, you may have students read whole passages from the course text and write answers to typical questions asked in the course (short answer, essay, etc.). This is another way to judge how well students can read the text and relate it to the course.

Referral: Reading Lab/Skills Center

Student:_____   Instructor:_____

Course: _____   Date:_____

This student would like assistance in reading and studying

the course text, which is _____.

Please assist the student in previewing the assigned

chapters and in understanding vocabulary related to con-

cepts. Thank you.

Figure 4.4

Step 5: Make referrals where necessary. Although your adoption of the strategies that appear in this book will help students to read your course material, you may feel, based on the assessment of students' skills and reading assignments, that some students can use even more assistance. In such cases do not hesitate to solicit the aid of your school's reading specialist. A sample referral form is given in Figure 4.4.

In summary, for some students the language and format of your textbook or technical articles may be difficult to understand. By using strategies presented in this book, however, you can reduce frustration and increase comprehension. Yet to determine whether such strategies are necessary, you will need to assess your students' reading abilities in relation to your specific reading assignments. The steps in this strategy should help you make such an assessment.

Part II

Strategies for Helping Students Write for Content Courses

5 | Developing Brief Writing Tasks

Overview

Recent nationwide attention to writing has emphasized its central role in learning. Writing down an idea solidifies it and gives it shape, opens it to inspection and change. Through writing we think, informally jotting down a few words here and there, a sentence a bit further on, a paragraph or a page as an idea develops.

Because of our own academic background, however, we may equate writing in our classes with the kinds of assignments we ourselves pursued amid stacks of books in a library. Yet finding student writers with weak skills, we may turn away in frustration from such assignments. How can anyone with problems in writing skills do the research and analysis needed for a long investigatory paper, we wonder.

Although we do tend to think of writing as long efforts, in fact most of us regularly ask students to write short pieces which, because of their brevity, often do not incline us to think of them as writing "assignments." These short writing assignments present themselves frequently throughout the term's work. When students write a summary or a short review or a critique or a report, when they write a thoughtful response to a homework question, when they write an essay in an examination or on a quiz, they face brief writing tasks. Although most of these tend to promote somewhat more sustained written responses than the responses to the *reading guide questions* presented in Strategy 13, some of these guide questions, too, may be thought of as brief writing tasks. For example, a guide question such as "Analyze the structure of the Hispanic family in New York" may draw out a few pages from the student. Other guide questions, on the other hand, may require only a sentence or two in response.

In these and other brief writing tasks there are many benefits for student and teacher alike. Several short assignments instead of one or two long ones allow for incremental learning of content, and whatever comments you make about the presentation of ideas can serve writers on the *next* try, where they can apply your suggestions in a new context. Frequent writing makes the student familiar with the elements of your subject, because anyone who works often and in varied modes with the language and thought patterns demanded by a discipline has a good chance to learn the subject matter successfully. And for the instructor, the brief writing task ends the nightmare we all share of suffocating in paperwork. It takes much less time to read and to critique several short assignments—three or four one- or two-page efforts, say—than to plod through term papers of ten or fifteen pages each.

To be sure, there are benefits for students who prepare long research projects (and Strategy 7 addresses ways to guide and improve the class performance there too), but other kinds of writing also have great value for instructional goals. Because of its importance in most courses, the brief writing assignment is worth considering first among strategies for stimulating good student writing. As with any writing assignment, even the brief one must be carefully planned and expectations must be clearly defined so that students understand fully the tasks you set for them. Explaining each activity with precise instructions—your efforts with "cue words" (see below) will be very helpful here—encourages students to meet your goals for short assignments as well as for long papers or for observation reports (see Strategies 7 and 8). You will explore all these typical writing exercises in turn as you examine the strategies in this section. This first strategy, however, focuses upon the steps involved in the preparation of clear and challenging brief writing assignments for your class.

Strategy 5: Developing Brief Writing Tasks

Step 1: Identify the task. Review your course syllabus to determine a point at which a brief writing assignment would help students learn content for an early unit in your course. You may want to choose an examination question, an assignment to write a report, a reaction paper, a critique, or simply an assignment that calls for a sustained response to a series of questions regarding one or more required readings from the textbook.

Step 2: Review "cue words." Cue words are words that clue students in to the type of information that they should be looking for or the kind of thinking that they should be doing. All teachers do not agree on the exact definitions of these various words. Most students do not even think to ask what is meant by these words; they just assume that they know. It is not difficult, then, for confusion to occur—a student will offer an example when a definition has been asked for or a description in place of an interpretation. To avoid this mix-up, it is essential that teachers share *their definitions* of cue words with students. Below are some examples of common cue words and their possible definitions. Note, however, that the particular needs of your students, your course, and your discipline may suggest refinements of these definitions and/or additional cue words.

Cue Words	*Definition*
agree/disagree	to consent or differ in opinion
analyze	to examine the parts of

compare/contrast	to give similarities or differences
define	to state the meaning of a word; to give the distinguishing characteristics of
describe	to give details based on sensory observations
explain	to give reasons for; to make comprehensible; to account for
illustrate	to give examples
list/identify	to give a series of
name state	to point out
paraphrase or restate	to tell in one's own words

As you reviewed these cue words, you may have noticed that a hierarchy exists among some of these words and the level of thinking they elicit. For example, students may need to "identify" or "define" certain concepts before they can "analyze" or "compare/contrast" them. This embedding of tasks within tasks will need to be kept in mind both as you work for clarity in phrasing your assignment and as you explain your expectations to students.

Step 3: Clarify the task. After identifying the task and reviewing the types of words that are likely to clue students in to the task involved in an assignment, you can formulate a specific brief assignment to reflect the task. Use the cue words that elicit the precise information you want, and *write* out a *single* statement or a question that is brief and clear and that identifies the exact information required. Here are some sample writing tasks developed for a number of different courses. Note both the use of cue words and the clarity and brevity of the assignments; note, too, how the cue words signal both the level of thinking about the topic and the type of writing demanded of the student.

List some of the changes brought about by the Industrial Revolution in England.

Compare the advantages of running and of swimming in terms of a person's physical health.

Explain the reasons for the current shift in population to America's Sun Belt.

Illustrate the ways families can meet the high cost of a college education for their children.

Define sociobiology.

Analyze a small group to which you currently belong.

Step 4: Make the task concrete and challenging. Now add any special conditions that will challenge students to produce their best efforts. You might try defining a persona for the writer or insisting upon a particular audience for the work or merely creating an imaginative wrinkle in the terms of the project. Notice the refinements in some of the assignments below, and contrast them with the original statements.

> You are an aging citizen of England in 1895. *List* some changes brought about in your personal and working life by the Industrial Revolution.

> Prepare a lecture for a group of business executives in which you *compare* and *contrast* running and swimming as exercises that improve a person's physical well-being.

> *Explain* in an essay to shopkeepers and to owners of small businesses the reasons for the current shift in population to America's Sun Belt.

> Write one paragraph to *illustrate* to a working, middle-class parent whether or not it is possible to beat the high cost of college. Support your opinion with specific factual detail.

> Write a page in which you *define* sociobiology for students in this class.

> *Identify* and *analyze* the roles you take in a small group to which you currently belong.

Step 5: Define the terms in your assignment. Even if the cue words you use are familiar to students, define those words within your assignment so that there is no confusion about them. Go back to your task statement and add an explanation of the cue words, as the following indicate:

> Write a paper in which you *define* sociobiology. (*To define* means "to give the distinguishing characteristics of some work or idea.")

> Prepare a lecture for a group of business executives in which you *compare* and *contrast*—that is, state the likenesses and differences between—running and swimming as exercises that improve a person's physical well-being.

Step 6: Add to the statement of task any special instructions about form and content. Depending upon the assignment, of course, you can state any special requirements about this task. You might want to specify a required length. You might want to define a structure students can use handily. You might insist, for example, upon a clear statement in the essay of the writer's main idea (also called *thesis sentence, proposition,* or *proposal,* among other names). Good expository writing makes its point early and clearly, and you want to encourage students to produce such a statement.

Although general writing requirements distributed early in the term (see Strategy 15) can provide detailed information on format, instructions such as the following can make especially clear some of the instructor's expectations on a particular assignment.

Your essay should be about one typed page in length.

(or)

Be sure to write an introductory paragraph and a concluding paragraph along with the appropriate number of body paragraphs you need to make your point. Do not exceed two or three handwritten pages, however.

(or)

When you write this short essay, make sure that one sentence in your introduction tells exactly what the main point of your report is, the point that all the other paragraphs will try to support. Put a check in the margin next to that sentence.

(or)

Write only one paragraph of twelve to fifteen sentences. Your first sentence should state exactly what main point you want to make.

Step 7: Put all these steps together in a clear, precise, concise statement of task. Examine the various strands you have created thus far, and gather them together as a draft of an assignment that ultimately you will present to students. Read the draft over; edit it further for clarity and precision; remove any possible ambiguities. Present your statement *in writing* to the class. Here is a sample assignment:

Write one paragraph of about twelve or fifteen sentences in which you illustrate to a working, middle-class parent ways to meet the high costs of college today. (*To illustrate* means "to offer supporting examples.") In your first sentence be sure to tell exactly what main point you want to make about college costs. Then use specific factual details to support your position.

The more effort you take in writing out an assignment, in revising it for specificity and clarity, and in making it challenge the class, the better the results when you have to read and to evaluate papers. Additionally, the cautious drafting of the statement for a writing task mirrors the process you expect students to follow when they write responses to your assignment, and the more you practice that process, the more help and advice you can give to developing writers. Also, by being precise, you can help to alleviate some of the anxiety students feel when they face a writing task.

6 | Overseeing the Writing Process

Overview

Most people recognize the value of collaboration in writing. Anyone who has written an article, a story, a book, an essay, or even an advertisement in a newspaper realizes the benefits of getting feedback while preparing the piece. Academia, of course, is no exception. An essay submitted to a scholarly journal, for example, goes out for review; colleagues familiar with the subject of the paper read it and write comments about it; the journal editor suggests new directions in a cover letter or in the margins; and the writer of the paper in preparing another draft mulls over the advice, accepts a point for this page but rejects an idea for that one, expands a sentence here and adds a page or two there, deletes from the introduction an extraneous paragraph better served in an annotation, but holds fast in refusing to alter the conclusion. Finally, after publication, someone may write a letter or a review about the article or book, pointing out strengths and weaknesses in the work. Although many may smart at hostile or indifferent comments about their prose, most of us do appreciate the enormous benefits of friendly, enlightened responses to our work. Even with job-related writing such as letters, memos, and committee reports, we learn from what our colleagues suggest on successive drafts, more confident on the final copy than we might otherwise be. For collaboration opened our eyes to nuances in thought and style that we might never have noticed on our own.

Students, too, can benefit greatly from ongoing commentary on their work. And they need to know about the series of complicated steps required for effective writing, from the moment a task is defined (or defines itself), through drafts, to the execution and the submission of the final manuscript.

One of the best ways to help students develop as writers in your discipline, then, is to provide commentary at stages of writing *prior* to the final copy students will submit. Unfortunately, many teachers direct their energies at commenting on this last effort, where suggestions are lost because it is really too late for the writer to make changes. (Students can feel as helpless about reading comments at this stage as we can in reading criticism of a work we have already published or a report we have already submitted.) Few students rework a paper when a grade is on it. However, when we provide comments during prewriting efforts (see Strategy 6) or at early draft stages, students can put into practice a suggestion for improvement in form or in content as they turn drafts into final manuscripts. Looking at drafts or at outlines or other pre-writing materials in an effort to improve them, you can offer perceptive comments where they have the greatest force. And when you do come to write reactions on final drafts, you can build upon suggestions you made earlier, evaluating just how much students have advanced in their mastery of the material you have examined along the way.

There are many ways to guide students through the process of writing. One effective beginning is for instructors themselves to think about their own writing practices. It is helpful for students to know how *you* operate as a writer, and it is helpful for them to see what the pieces *you* produce look like as you move along to write, ultimately, an acceptable product. For when you consider your own habits as a writer, you can advise students not on the basis of rules set out in a writing text (rules few of us follow exactly), but rather, more productively, on the basis of your own experience. For example, when the class writes, many teachers insist upon the formal outline as a crucial step in composing; yet when they examine their own efforts, they discover the limited usefulness of such outlines. In fact, not many writers do outline in the way most of us have been taught to. We might group our ideas informally before we write, certainly; or we might use an outline to check the logic of something we have already written; but as a formative stage in the writing process many find the full outline of doubtful value. The point is that only self-examination of your own writing patterns can produce insights about what really works for you and, by extension, about what might work for the class.

The steps in the following strategy explore typical stages in the writing process and suggest ways both to use your own efforts as a writer to help students produce better prose and to provide commentary when they most need it.

Strategy 6: Overseeing the Writing Process

Step 1: Review the steps in the writing process and check off those you yourself usually take. Any writing task proceeds through a number of stages, often overlapping and interacting with each other. It is important for you to review those stages and to become aware of which ones work for you so that you have a clear sense of how writers in general and how your students in particular can progress through a task. Not everyone uses all of these, of course, but some characteristic stages through which a piece of writing may develop include:

1. Thinking about the subject by brainstorming either to identify or discover a topic or to explore one that has been identified; using free association, jottings, or timed writing to record *any*

    phrases, clauses, or sentences that come to mind about the topic; organizing ideas with simple grouping efforts or with scratch outlines before drafting an essay; or following any other activities that loosen writers up and allow them to explore their topics.

2. Limiting the topic.
3. Recalling, observing, researching, or notetaking (or a combination of these).
4. Making a list of main points and subpoints or outlining material formally.
5. Writing the first draft.
6. Writing the second and subsequent drafts.
7. Writing the final manuscript.

Many teachers call the steps a writer takes before preparing a rough draft *prewriting*. It is a helpful term, especially for beginners who mistakenly skip stages 1–4 above. To be sure, each of these stages presents its own obstacles, which writers learn to overcome only through frequent practice.

Step 2: For the brief writing assignment you developed in the last strategy, perform prewriting activities that help you explore your topic before you write. Little will show so clearly the problems students face in producing an essay for your course than your own attempt to respond to your own writing assignment. Hence, for one of the writing tasks you will assign to students, produce *on paper* samples of prewriting that you feel help *you* write effectively. Do free association, brainstorming, timed writing, a scratch outline, jottings, or a formal outline (choose one or several of these)—in short, any activities that can loosen you up when you write or that can help you clarify or organize your thoughts. Do not yet produce a draft.

Below is a sample of a prewriting effort by an instructor in a literature course. The assignment for the class appears first:

Writing Assignment

    Most people at one time or another in their lives like to play (real or imaginary) games. In your first reading assignment, "The Most Dangerous Game," Richard Connell, the author, takes this common need and habit and elevates it into a passion. His big game hunter, General Zaroff, turns from hunting lions and tigers and other large animals to hunting human beings in order to increase both the challenge and the risks of his effort.

For your first written assignment (400–750 words), which is to be based in part on Connell's story, do the following:

1. *Identify* (point out) a game you particularly like to play, and tell *why* you like to play it. The *why* will form your *main point*.

2. *Describe* (give details in visual words) the game's features.

3. *Provide illustrations* (give examples) of the difficulties and/or dangers of the game, and tell the reader how you feel about them.

4. *Compare* and *contrast* (give similarities and differences) between your approach and those of other people you know who also play the same game.

5. *Compare* and *contrast* (give similarities and differences) between the game that you play and the one described in the story.

It is recommended that the answer to Question 1 form your introduction, that the answers to Questions 2 to 4 form the *body* of your essay, and that the answer to Question 5 form your conclusion. Other organizational methods are of course possible, but whatever you do, be sure that the format you choose does include the three building blocks of the essay: an *introduction*, a *body*, and a *conclusion*.

Prewriting: "The Most Dangerous Game"

Electronic games

Odyssey Video (tennis on TV) Game—has been played by my son Paul and me

Suggests

    A. Need for *competition* (statement of challenge)

    B. Aggressiveness

    C. Digital dexterity (the need for it in the game)

    D. Age-old battle (at testing between father and son)

End of intro?

Although we rarely play anymore (my son having turned fifteen and moved on to the sophistication of computers and their more complicated pleasures), we still sometimes in a moment of regression (nostalgia?) return to the game to relax.

How to play

    A. Explain knobs
        1. to activate play

starter
placing the net
ball speed

2. actually to play game
movement of ball
movement of player to and from net
movement of player along net

B. How to win

Step 3: From your prewriting efforts now produce on paper at least one page of a first draft for this assignment. Write a rough draft now for the assignment you will make to students. Because you will share your draft with the class, leave intact everything you produce here. Do not erase words or sentences you reject as you write—cross them out instead. In response to his assignment for the literature class, an instructor produced the rough draft in Figure 6.1.

Step 4: From your original one-page rough draft of your own assignment, produce a second draft—and whatever subsequent drafts your own writing practices demand—as well as a final draft for that page. Work your rough draft over in whatever way you ordinarily might in order to make it ready for recopying into a final manuscript. If you add, shift, or delete words or sentences, use ink or pencil in a color different from what you used for your rough draft; or cut and paste sections, as you ordinarily might, in order to save time from having to write yet another draft. Remember that you will be saving all the pieces of this writing as samples for students, and it is important for the class to see all your time-saving tricks too. After you have worked on your rough draft, however, you may need to rewrite it in any case so that the ideas are easier for you to read. Again, keep whatever drafts you make. Once you are satisfied with your draft, rewrite (or retype) it as a final manuscript.

The final draft of the first page or so of the essay that responds to the literature assignment appears in Figure 6.2.

Step 5: Arrange the pages you have just produced for use in connection with your own short writing assignment. Label the various pieces you have just produced: prewriting, draft 1, draft 2 (if you have one; draft 3 and 4 as needed), and final manuscript. Decide on a way to share those pieces with the class. You might choose to make transparencies and to use the overhead projector in order to show the class what you produced, or you might choose to duplicate your prewriting efforts and drafts for each member of the class to have.

Step 6: Develop an activity for overseeing the prewriting stage in connection with your first writing assignment. To help the class in gener-

A Game That Counts

During the last two years or so, Paul, my son, and I have
been played a miniature form of ~~television,~~ tennis, using a TV and a signal
~~playing~~ board manufactured by the makers of Odyssey 500 House
Video ~~game~~ Game. ~~The~~ Our sessions, which are quite lengthy, ~~ask~~ are
of interest for many reasons, perhaps most prominently a not-so-
subtle form of testing between father and son. Although we
rarely play any more (my son having turned fifteen and moved on
to the ~~sophisti~~ more-sophisticated pleasures ~~provided~~ offered by
computers), we sometimes return, in a moment of regression or
perhaps nostalgia, to the older and simpler ~~pleasure of game~~
form of relaxation.

Three switches start the game going. One starts the play,
another places the net, another fixes the speed of the ball. To
play you have to use three other knobs. One knob regulates the
~~ball~~ movement of the ball, another ~~moves~~ places the player close or
further away from the net (left or right on the TV screen), and
a third knob moves the player along the net (vertically up and
down on the TV screen). ~~To win the winner~~ The first player to
earn twenty-one points wins.

Figure 6.1

ating ideas about an assignment, in finding suitable topics for it, and in avoiding the pitfalls of writing about topics that are too general, develop a strategy that helps you explore *prewriting* as an aid to completing your assignment successfully.

You might review with students various prewriting techniques, allowing different students to share their own favorite kinds of prewriting efforts. Here is the point at which you demonstrate and explain the kind of prewriting you did for one of your own assignments. You

A Game That Counts

During the last two years or so, my son Paul and I have played a miniature form of tennis, using a TV screen and a signal board manufactured by the makers of the <u>Odyssey</u> <u>500</u> <u>House</u> <u>Video</u> <u>Game</u>. Our sessions, which are sometimes quite lengthy, are of interest for many reasons, perhaps most prominently suggesting the excitement and challenge of competition, the relief that is provided by a "safe" outlet for aggressive behavior, the satisfactions (or frustrations) that come with the application of physical skills, and, finally, a not so subtle form of testing between father and son. Although we rarely play any more (my son having turned fifteen and moved on to the more sophisticated pleasures offered by computers), we sometimes return in a moment of regression or perhaps nostalgia, to the older and simpler form of relaxation.

The game itself is much like ordinary tennis but is activated by three switches, one which starts the play, another which places the net, and a third which adjusts the speed of the ball. There are also three knobs which must be used constantly if the players are to be successful in their efforts. One knob regulates the movement of the ball, another places the player closer to or farther away from the net (left to right on the TV screen), and a third knob moves the player along the net (vertically up and down on the TV screen). The first player to get twenty-one points, based on the miscalculations or other misfortunes of an opponent, wins the game.

Figure 6.2

might create an in-class activity that will allow students practice in generating topics. Or you might provide an exercise that will help students limit them. For example, you might want to review the prewriting stage by developing an activity such as one of these:

Thinking About a Topic

One way to think about a topic in writing is to write your assigned subject on the top of the page and then to write down a series of questions that the topic arouses, questions such as, but not limited to, those reporters ask—Who? What? When? Where? Why? How? Then try to answer those questions or to figure out how you might find answers to them.

Timed Writing

If your topic for this paper is *education* and you don't know where to begin, for ten minutes try writing nonstop everything that comes into your mind when you hear the word *education*. Keep writing, even if you have to keep stating, "I don't know what to write." Fill up a page with prose.

Limiting a Topic

To limit your topic, try to narrow it down in stages. You might use columns such as those below in which you limit progressively an overly broad area into one more suitable for writing.

Too Broad	Still Broad	Less Broad	Specific Enough
Teaching	New teaching techniques	New techniques for teaching special children	New techniques for teaching deaf children

Outlining

Show the class a rough outline you produced for your writing assignment. You might ask students to discuss their impressions of the usefulness of outlining.

Whichever procedure you choose in a prewriting effort, your own conviction about it as a successful step to take in the writing process will convince the class of its usefulness more than anything else.

Step 7: Develop a way to provide reactions to students about their prewriting efforts. To provide students with comments on how effectively they have limited the topic (if you encourage a free choice of topic) and how they are progressing in developing it, decide when and how you will check on progress at the early stages of topic development. Announce to the class whatever procedure you will follow.

You might wish to choose one of these approaches to use with your class:

> Before you begin work on this assignment, come to see me during my office hours so that you can explain how you will develop your topic.

(or)

> Write down your topic choice on this slip of paper. I'll read each one aloud in class, and we will discuss the topics together.

(or)

> Meet in groups to think about and discuss your topics. By next Monday, each person should submit for approval one clear sentence stating the main idea of his or her paper. I'll return these, with comments and suggestions, before you begin research.

Step 8: Provide samples and require a rough draft. To minimize anxiety about producing good written content, provide samples of past students' successful papers as you make the assignment. You will have to start a file and to collect good student writing over the years to help you achieve this goal. In the meantime, share with students what *you* wrote in response to the assignment you are making. (If you produced a finished paper, so much the better.) In considering samples with the class, make sure that you direct attention to the strengths of the essays and that you explain why the papers succeed. You might read them aloud; you might have one or two students read the papers to the class while everyone else listens and takes notes; you might ask small groups to consider a good paper and to react to it; or you might duplicate one strong essay, or parts of one, for students to take home for reference as they write their assignments.

Then, in keeping with your general goal of helping students take their writing through a series of steps, *require* the production of a rough draft and ensure that students receive commentary on it. This commentary may come from you, from students' peers, or from a combination of these sources.

Feedback is an important part of the writing process, and arranging for students to have comments on written work before it is evaluated with a grade is especially important so that students improve the final treatment of the paper. But it is also important for students to receive comments when you evaluate a completed, final piece of work with a grade. Comments on a graded paper may be brief and succinct, for they tend to judge a given piece of work more than they tend to suggest new directions in another draft. Yet even remarks on a graded paper can help students when they attempt a new assignment.

Some of the following steps suggest ways to write productive commentary.

Step 9: Review the differences between descriptive and evaluative comments and the effects each type may have upon students' progress as writers. Whether it is you who provides feedback on writing or whether it is students who do it, two basic questions should guide any remarks about students' papers: *What is the writer trying to say? How well has he or she succeeded in saying it?* The first question objectively focuses attention on the assignment, on whether or not the writer addresses it in the paper, and on how clearly the writer has stated his or her main point. The second question focuses on language and form, on evidence and detail. As the reader frames sentences that address those questions, comments should, as much as possible, describe objectively what appears on the page. Specific objective descriptions are much more valuable than general subjective judgments because the latter, especially when they are negative or ironic or angry, can impede further work on the paper. Even when subjective comments do pinpoint a specific change—usually they do not, however—students easily can become paralyzed by the tone of subjective remarks. (If you make a subjective comment, try to make it a positive one, then.) In the following, compare the subjective comments at the left with the more objective remarks on the right, and think about the effects each type would have on a writer.

Subjective (general)	Objective (descriptive and specific)
• This is a poor introduction.	• Your introduction lacks a thesis sentence.
• Your writing skills are very weak.	• Your paper has several sentence fragments and spelling errors.
• You obviously do not know how to write an essay.	• This essay has neither an introduction nor a conclusion. And paragraphs developing your main points require supporting detail drawn from reliable sources.
• What a ridiculous point!	• You must make clear how you reach this conclusion. As it stands now, no evidence in the paper supports this point.

It is clear that a writer is bound to take more seriously the sentences on the right. In making comments, then, the reader should aim here to see himself or herself as a trusted, friendly, yet astute advisor, one whose advice requires serious thought. Hence you have to use language carefully so that you say clearly what you mean and so that you avoid insulting students or showing anger or frustration at their efforts.

Step 10: Develop a collaborative situation in which students offer comments on each other's drafts. A useful strategy is to arrange for peer feedback. Put students into groups: review the terms of the assignment; then ask each writer to read his or her draft aloud while the rest of the group takes notes on strengths and weaknesses in the expression of ideas. To guide constructive collaboration, you will find it helpful to prepare with the class a checklist of pointers to consider in reacting to drafts each time around. Some items you might want to put on the checklist in order to focus students' comments to include directions about the main point of the paper, about the clarity of language, and about the logical use of supporting data to make a point. There are others, of course, based on content as well as on form. The important thing to remember is that commentators understand that their remarks be specific and, as much as possible, that they be descriptive rather than evaluative.

After each reader is finished, group members may discuss the draft with the author. Or you can arrange for groups of three to read papers and then to *write* commentary for their colleagues. With this plan each student takes home two critiques to guide revisions. Not only does collaboration of this sort call students' attention to the quality of the writing of their peers, but it also makes students attentive to subject matter. Interaction with a collaborative group that considers the ideas of an essay and their implications in terms of the discipline produces powerful learning indeed.

Step 11: Develop a means for providing your own comments on students' drafts. Your strategy may be to collect rough drafts and to write down questions or to make helpful suggestions about content. Or you might discuss drafts of portions of them in individual conferences with students. Commenting on drafts does add to your workload, certainly; but ironically, it also cuts it down. With nonevaluative comments that suggest new avenues for exploration or that guide students to productive change on their drafts, you can avoid making extensive comments on final copies, where instead you can concentrate on judging the paper.

With the goal of being descriptive and not evaluative, you can provide helpful direction by raising a question right alongside the passage that stimulated your reaction. Thus you direct attention to a specific line in the paper that needs reworking. Questions have great value in that they do not judge, but rather call for further information that the reader needs and that the writer overlooked. Questions such as these can lead the writer to produce change:

Is this repetition deliberate? If so, what is your reason for it?

What do you mean by *neurosis* in this paragraph?

Why do you offer no support for this point?

Descriptive, objective comments or comments that suggest specific changes or that praise the writer's efforts are helpful:

Excellent image!

Your paragraphs rarely exceed three or four sentences.

I've checked off examples of informal language. Change them into standard written English.

In your next draft strive for more details. Your main point in paragraph two needs more support.

Combine these three sentences into one for a clearer, smoother paragraph.

Another way to help a writer develop a strong manuscript is to call attention to major errors. The interaction of content and form—the *what* and the *how* of any written work—is essential to any good writing, and students need direction in both areas.

About errors, however, you have to be really careful, because pointing them out at very early draft stages is a mistake. When writers are still developing their ideas, they need to focus on logic and on clarity of expression and not on spelling or on errors with subjects and verbs. Comments on first drafts generally should avoid discussion of language errors altogether. However, when students submit a draft beyond the first—and certainly when they submit their final manuscripts—you do need to call attention to mistakes.

But you do not want to correct those mistakes. What is wrong with an instructor's correcting a student's error or with making other kinds of editorial changes on students' papers? In the first place, the students themselves should be the only ones to alter, finally, the language they have produced. It is simply a matter of courtesy not to slash out words and to write in others in someone else's prose. Next, the prose produced by the instructor's editorial changes is the instructor's prose and no longer represents the student's own thinking. Finally, students must learn to be their own editors and to find their own mistakes and infelicities of phrasing.

Thus the recommendation here is for you to call attention to problems and errors but not to make changes. Instead, identify problems in the margin next to the lines in which they appear, or raise questions about choices made by students in regard to language or syntax. For example:

> You made two subject-verb agreement errors on this page.
>
> Why did you use this word?
>
> Why did you use a period here instead of a comma?

Some instructors circle or underline errors on the line so that students know which words need correction. To point out mistakes, others use conventional marking symbols with which students usually have had some experience in past English courses. (If you do use marking symbols, be sure to provide in your statement of your general writing requirements—see Strategy 15—a list of those symbols along with explanations of their meaning and examples of how to correct them.) Other instructors point out only one or two kinds of errors on each paper so that the class focuses as a group on a limited number of special problems.

Perhaps the most helpful kind of comment, both on early and intermediate drafts *and* on final manuscripts, is the statement you make at the end of the paper. Let your comments there reflect your concern with language form *and* content, and always summarize positive elements in a paper (no matter how poor the paper) before you zero in on the errors. Here is a sample final comment on a student's draft:

> Your definition of *ex post facto* states the major qualities implied by that term. The example you gave from your own experience helps clarify your point. But you gave only one example and drew no support from expert testimony, a requirement for this paper. Why? Your frequent misspellings and errors in sentence structure distract the reader and make it hard to focus on your good ideas. Try for at least half the number of mistakes on your next paper. Go to the Writing Center for help with your errors.

Notice how these comments highlight the strengths in the essay before moving to its weaknesses. Notice, too, the specific, objective description ("But you gave only one example . . ."; "Your frequent misspellings . . .") and the suggestions for improvement ("Try for at least half . . .").

A comment at the end of the paper is a summation of your concerns. Questions and remarks along the way in the margins help lead up to that final comment, so that its placement on the last page of the essay is more logical than on the cover sheet, a place many instructors, without thinking, will choose for their criticisms. If you make comments on the same paper on which you also intend to record a grade, write down the grade *after* you write down the comments. Otherwise, students tend to focus on their marks alone and to disregard whatever verbal analysis you have provided.

Step 12: Anticipate editorial problems with an exercise designed to focus attention on predominant errors. Develop an activity to help students locate typical errors before you collect final manuscripts for grading. For example, a brief exercise like one of these serves nicely:

> Before you hand in your papers today, take these next ten minutes to do a final proofreading of your manuscript. Look especially for the kinds of errors you made the last time. Use your pocket dictionaries to check any words whose spelling you are unsure of.

> In regard to this assignment on nutrition look at the spelling of these words that might show up in your papers. Students in the past have frequently misspelled these words. I've underlined the trouble-spots so that you can avoid the errors: polysaccharides, cellulose, enzymes, photosynthesis, protein.

Step 13: Require students' responses to comments and corrections on final drafts. If you and other people in the class make extensive comments and guide corrections on early drafts, you can see just how students accommodate your suggestions on subsequent drafts of the same paper. This is especially true if your comments raise questions or suggest a course of action. The final manuscript, then, should represent each writer's best effort after collaboration with colleagues.

If you reserve comments for final drafts only, however, you want to assure students' responses to your written suggestions too. (Even if you do not comment on drafts, some problems also may show up on final copies, and you will want students to attempt to correct these problems before the next paper.)

You may choose from a number of approaches in guiding students to respond to comments and corrections.

- *Require rewrites.* If students write on one side of each page only, they can use the blank reverse side to revise phrases, sentences, or paragraphs. If you have guided the class through successive drafts, there is no need to require fully rewritten papers after you grade them finally.
- *Require corrections.* Students should correct any error you have pointed out in language, grammar, or syntax; and you should check to see that they make appropriate corrections. Suggest that students use pencil or a second color of ink to make changes directly above their mistakes. In that way, when you collect the graded papers, you can look quickly for corrections.
- *Encourage error inventories.* By requiring that students keep

														Date	
														Title of composition	
														RO	
														Frag	
														Agr	Grammar
														Vb	
														Pro	
														Ms	
														Cap	Mechanics
														It	
														Abbr	
														,	
														;	
														'	
														"	
														./	
														!/	Punctuation
														?/	
														:/	
														–/	
														( )/	
														-/	
														Sp	Spelling and
														Voc	vocabulary
														Us	Diction
														Ef	
														Var	
														Ord	
														//	Strong sentences
														mm	
														Dang	
														¶	
														¶ Det	Paragraphs and
														¶ Dev	essays
														E	

Figure 6.3 From Harvey S. Wiener, *Creating Compositions,* 2nd ed. New York: McGraw-Hill. Copyright © 1981 by Harvey S. Wiener. Used with permission of the McGraw-Hill Book Company and the author.

individual records of their own errors from paper to paper, you help each writer focus on problems *before* the next effort. Thus, looking at an inventory of problems identified on the last paper and recorded in a notebook or on a chart such as the one in Figure 6.3, students have a chance to prevent the recurrence of similar errors.

Step 14: Whenever possible, encourage students to see each other's final papers. As you know, peer collaboration is extremely valuable as the student produces successive drafts. After papers are turned in and graded as final manuscripts, too, it is helpful to share the work of the class. Here, again, is a chance to expand students' contact with subject matter, this time by providing an opportunity for the class to develop fresh insights from each other and to learn firsthand what the hard work of their colleagues can produce. To show how well some students have responded to the assignments, try to provide opportunities for examining papers written by members of the class, papers that meet your goals admirably so that the reasons for achievement become clear. Thus you might

- Have papers (or excerpts from them) read aloud in small groups or to the whole class as students listen for specific points (the originality of thought, the quality of organization in the paper, the strength of supporting detail, and so on); or duplicate portions of successful papers on transparencies for the overhead projector.
- Ask students to submit two copies of their papers and, arranging details with the school library, require students to read a number of papers you reserve there.
- Ask students to make two or three photocopies of brief assignments; divide the class into small groups and allow peers to write comments on papers and then to discuss them.
- Arrange with your department chair to produce a newspaper or a journal of student writing from your course.

Step 15: Develop a brief exercise to highlight major errors if students show frequent serious problems in their writing. A further way to advance skills for those students just learning to write for your discipline is to call attention to major problems. You may also do this by providing a brief exercise that highlights them for a given assignment you have graded. Such an exercise also helps students to prevent those errors in the future and to recognize that individual errors generally fall into recognizable patterns. It may be helpful to use one of the techniques suggested below:

- Oral dictation
- Sentences duplicated from papers and shared with the class
- A paragraph of student writing for class analysis

Thus one exercise you give might look something like this:

Look at the excerpts from paragraphs from several of your last papers. Which sentences provide details successfully? Which sentences do not make their point adequately because of insufficient details? What might you add to improve the sentences?

I am going to read several excerpts from your papers. Write them correctly now on a blank sheet of paper.

1. French communism.
2. It was all right.
3. Use *I* or *me* correctly in the blank space in this sentence: Between my husband and _____ we can earn $22,000.

By guiding students through the writing process, you will notice a marked improvement in the way they write for your course and, in turn, they should begin to experience writing as a tool to understanding your discipline.

Students need more than a grade on a written page: they need recognition of their efforts and of their strengths as writers and as thinkers, and they need concrete guidance for improvement in areas that show weakness. With your comments, you influence correctness and clarity, certainly; but you influence content and critical thinking also, merely by directing the writer to pursue a particular line of reasoning, to consider an alternative point, or to suggest ways to improve sentence logic.

7 | Creating Research Assignments

Overview

As assignments go, nothing perhaps is more familiar to the instructor than the formal paper. There are many formats for it. However, each formal paper generally involves research in the library on some clearly defined topic; it presents a thesis and offers support by citing evidence drawn from authoritative sources; and it provides careful documentation for those sources. Some papers center on analyses or reviews of paintings, performances, poems, novels, plays, or works of nonfiction. Whatever the form, however, the formal paper allows the student to concentrate attention on a limited aspect of the discipline. And perhaps more than any other task, this assignment requires the students to perform as professionals in that discipline.

Yet for students both unfamiliar with your subject and inexperienced as writers, the long paper can be an undecipherable puzzle. After all, although researchers in different academic areas follow many similar steps and use many similar techniques, each subject nonetheless makes its own special demands on the student. And teachers vary in their requirements and expectations. It is essential, therefore, that you let the class know exactly what you want by delineating—in writing—the steps students must take to produce the kind of paper you want them to produce.

Anywhere from five to ten pages or more, extended papers that require a student's close attention over a period of time—especially those assignments requiring research or field work or experimentation (see Strategy 8) integrated into a single essay—demand that you pay considerable attention to preparation for the task. So that students have a complete understanding of what you want in such a paper, it is wise to prepare careful instructions for distribution to the class. The following strategy suggests the steps to take in identifying and in explaining the various elements of a long assignment so that students can complete it successfully and can learn important content from it.

Strategy 7: Creating Research Assignments

Step 1: State the assignment clearly. Follow the same steps you followed in preparing a statement for a brief writing activity (identify and clarify the writing task; make it concrete and challenging; define key terms—

see Strategy 5). Once you are satisfied that your statement is clear and unambiguous and that it meets the guidelines explained on the pages named above, write it as the first item on a sheet of guidelines you will distribute to the class (see Strategy 15). Having this statement available makes it easier for students to respond precisely to the assignment *as you have written it* and reduces possible misunderstandings about it.

Step 2: Review the steps in producing written work. You want to remind students about the need to develop the idea for their paper—and its subsequent execution—through appropriate prewriting, drafting, and rewriting (see Strategy 6). Call attention to any *particular* stage you think merits special attention because of the nature of the assignment. (For long research projects in which students generate data, the outline, for example, can be of great value. In other cases outlines may be unnecessary and may not help very much. See Strategy 6.) Perhaps you might make a statement such as this on your page of instructions to students:

> Follow the steps you usually take in producing a written essay. Give each stage its due—brainstorming, outlining, writing the drafts, and so on. For this assignment, pay particular attention to the outline.

Step 3: Review the steps to take in doing research. If the assignment requires research, remind students of the steps to take when they do it. Although research procedures should be fully explained in the general writing requirements that you will distribute at the start of the course (see Strategy 15), a brief statement about research for this particular paper will help guide students through the special stages of investigation for this project. For example, you may wish to include a statement such as this one as part of your instructions:

> Remember to take time with each of the stages of research—limiting your topic, finding appropriate sources, taking notes, copying citations correctly for later documentation of sources, and so on.

Step 4: Name sources for finding appropriate bibliographic materials. For a project that requires research, identify one or more of the sources on which your discipline relies for names of appropriate books and/or articles. For students unfamiliar with your subject, this is important information to have. After you identify those you want to emphasize, prepare a statement that asks students to use them. For example, you might say something such as one of these:

> Use the *Social Science Index* to locate at least two articles on the subject.

(or)

Use the *General Science Index* and then *Biological Abstracts* for articles on your topic. (These indexes are in the third-floor reference collection of the college library.)

Step 5: Explain methods of citation. If your writing assignment requires research, prepare a statement that tells how you expect students to cite their sources. You might offer something such as one of these:

Cite your sources with footnotes. Use the format in the *MLA Handbook for Writers of Research Papers, Theses, and Dissertations* (available in the bookstore and in the reserve room of the college library).

(or)

Prepare a bibliography using the format recommended by the American Psychological Association.

(or)

For this assignment do not use footnotes or endnotes. Name your sources within the sentences of your paper itself, by integrating citations smoothly in the essay.

Example: John Rawls, in his essay "Justice as Fairness," *The Philosophical Review*, 67 (1958), 166–7, says...

Step 6: Provide any special instructions about form and content. In Strategy 15 you will see how to develop materials that explain your general requirements for all written work. However, for the long assignment a brief statement about manuscript preparation or about any special requirements for this paper will reinforce earlier instructions and will allow you to comment on special features demanded by the format of this report. Such a statement of special instructions should be included on the handout for students. For example, you might write something such as this:

Research projects should be in the range of five to ten pages. Type all final manuscripts neatly. Arrange your work in this order:

1. Title page.
2. Acknowledgments page. (Name the students in the class who read drafts of your paper and who advised you on the project.)
3. Outline.
4. Research essay.
5. Bibliography.

Step 7: Focus on typical writing problems. In Strategy 6 you looked at some techniques for identifying for the class major problems beginning writers often face when they write. But because it is often overwhelming to concentrate for each paper on numerous significant errors, you might want to focus on one or two of them for each assignment. You probably have found in your students' papers problems that distract you when you read. Let students know in advance the kinds of errors that you want the class particularly to avoid. Write a statement for your page of instructions to students such as:

> When you revise your drafts, look carefully at your introductions this time. Your introduction should be a single paragraph, usually shorter than other paragraphs in your paper; and a thesis sentence in your introduction should state clearly your purpose in writing this paper. <u>Underline the thesis sentence in your introductory paragraph</u>.

(or)

> Check your papers carefully for spelling errors and for sentence fragments. Look at the list of symbols distributed to you along with the course syllabus.

Step 8: Encourage editorial care and hold students accountable for careful work. Identifying the problems you find distracting is only one step in any effort to help students reduce errors. To encourage the class to identify mistakes before submitting long papers and yet to minimize your role as editor (a role you should *not* have to assume), you want to offer practice in the kind of self-evaluation all writers must learn in order to locate and to correct problems in their work. Hence develop a system that requires editorial care and that places upon students the responsibility for locating errors on papers submitted for final evaluation.

You might simply remind the class about proofreading (see Strategy 6). You might collect rough and final drafts to see how students attended to responsibilities for changing words and sentences for clarity and correctness. You might ask the class to read their colleagues' rough drafts in small groups so that collaboration will produce editorial changes. Or after grading papers, you might return them to the class and then collect them again for a quick rechecking after students make revisions. Another possibility that some instructors find successful is to ask students to certify that they have watched out for errors; thus you might ask them to write a "contract" and to attach a signed certification to their papers. Certainly, a reasonable combination of these suggestions will help advance your goals for good writing in your subject.

Statements such as those appearing below will help you formulate your own:

Proofread your paper carefully, both your rough drafts and your final draft. Use a dictionary and your English handbook to check any words or sentences that look strange to you. When you hand in your final draft, attach your rough draft to it so that I can see how you corrected your own errors.

(or)

When I return these papers with suggestions for improvement, you must acknowledge my points and questions by responding to them in the margin and by correcting any mistakes I've indicated. To get credit for your work, you must correct all errors and resubmit your work at the session after I return the papers.

(or)

Prepare a statement like this as the last page of your paper (fill in the blanks): I have read over my paper carefully for errors in _____, _____, and _____ and have tried to correct them.

_____
Signature

Step 9: Guide efficient pacing. To guide pacing and to assure that students are developing their writing tasks with care and within a reasonable time frame, decide *which* of the various parts of the long writing assignment you will collect and *when* you will collect them. These steps help students avoid waiting for the last minute to begin their research and writing their papers under unrealistic deadlines. Prepare for the assignment sheet you will distribute, then, a statement to reflect a suggested schedule. Like the instructor who prepared the instructions below, you may find it helpful to examine students' work at different stages of this long assignment.

The following segments are due on the dates indicated below. Each segment will be returned with comments that you should use to help you construct the final paper:

1. Topic statement and notes on any one article you have read about your topic—March 1
2. Tentative bibliography and tentative thesis statement—March 15
3. Draft of outline—April 7
4. First draft of paper—April 21
5. Final manuscript—May 15

Do not be put off by what may *seem* like added work. You can look quickly at these different materials and can comment briefly on them. But the results on the final effort will prove to you once and for all that

Research Assignment: The Effects of Alcohol and Marijuana

I.   Assignment

      Write a research paper in which you compare the biological
      effects on the human body of alcohol and of marijuana.
      (To compare means "to show likenesses and differences.")

II.   Stages of Manuscript Preparation

      A.   Steps in Producing a Written Work

           Follow the steps you usually take in producing a written
           essay. Give each step its due: brainstorming (or
           other prewriting techniques), writing rough and final
           drafts, and so on. For this assignment, pay particular
           attention to the outline.

      B.   Steps in Doing Research

           1.   Remember to take time with each of the stages of
                research--limiting your topic, finding sources,
                taking notes, outlining, documenting sources, and
                so on. (See General Writing Requirements handout
                for a more detailed explanation of how to proceed
                in a research assignment.)

           2.   Use the General Science Index and Biological
                Abstracts to locate articles on the subject.
                Use a minimum of five articles that deal with
                marijuana or alcohol; at least two of these must
                be articles written in the last two years.

           3.   Cite sources by means of the APA format (the
                author-date method). For the correct format for
                documentation use the Publication Manual of the
                American Psychological Association (available in
                the bookstore and in the reserve room of the
                college library).

           4.   Prepare a bibliography by listing all citations
                on a separate page called "References." Use APA
                style for the correct format.

Figure 7.1

III. Special Considerations

    A. Format

Research projects should be in the range of five to six pages. Type all final manuscripts neatly. Arrange your work in this order.

      1. Title page
      2. Acknowledgments page (Name the students in the class who read drafts of your paper and who advised you on the project.)
      3. Outline
      4. Research essay
      5. Bibliography (References)

    B. Editing

      1. When you revise your drafts, look carefully at your introduction this time. Your introduction should be a single paragraph usually shorter than other paragraphs in your paper; and a thesis sentence in your introduction should state clearly your purpose in writing this paper. <u>Underline the thesis sentence in your introductory paragraph</u>.

      2. Proofread your paper carefully, both your rough drafts and your final draft. Use a dictionary and your English handbook to check any words or sentences that look strange to you. When you hand in your final draft, attach your rough draft to it so that I can see how you corrected your own errors.

IV. Schedule

The following segments are due on the dates indicated below. Each segment will be returned with comments that you should use to help you construct the final paper:

1. Topic statement and notes on any one article you have read about your topic - March 1
2. Tentative bibliography (reference page) and tentative thesis statement - March 15
3. Draft of outline - April 7
4. First draft of paper - April 21
5. Final manuscript - May 15

Figure 7.1 (continued)

whatever time you give students during the stages of invention will improve results enormously and will, finally, save you time in evaluating the end product. On the basis of an assignment schedule such as the one above, some teachers ask students to prepare their own calendar to indicate when they will perform each research task. Students must submit the calendars early in the term.

Step 10: Collect the various statements you have produced so far and create a page of guidelines for the long paper. All the steps you have taken until now should converge in a written page of guidelines that clarify for students the requirements of a single paper. In preparing these guidelines, try to keep the instructions to not much more than a page or two, and organize the information so that students can see easily what you expect. Your set of guidelines might look like the one presented in Figure 7.1.

8 | **Assigning Field and Laboratory Reports**

Overview

Traditionally, papers based on primary and secondary sources in print make up a major part of students' written work for college. Yet many disciplines, as you know, depend heavily upon field or laboratory research. In many of their courses students must sharpen the skill of firsthand observation, must describe what careful observation reveals, must explain and sometimes evaluate observed phenomena, and, finally, must write up findings in a clear and logical report. Researchers in the pure and natural sciences and in the social sciences and the humanities will often write from data gathered in the laboratory or in the field or at museums or public agencies. Certainly, in the acquisition of knowledge, writing about firsthand observation plays a central role. Thus, although the completion of a paper tied to library research might be helpful to the art student, for example, another common assignment in an art course is a report based on a personal analysis of a painting or a piece of sculpture. A human services course, to take another case, might require students to write about observations at community centers offering treatment to patients. Then, too, a science course might require students to write up an experiment, recounting their observations and conclusions. For all these kinds of activities the students' firsthand reporting is the foundation for a written prose record of the experience.

This strategy suggests steps for developing materials to help students whose written work is a means of demonstrating an understanding of field or laboratory research. No substitute for long or short writing assignments explained in earlier strategies, the observation report is yet another kind of writing task to help students gain mastery of a subject.

Of course, every discipline has its own tested methods of collecting data, and so it is not the intention in suggesting strategies to insist on any particular method absolutely. Further, many students will develop their own creative approaches to the challenge of recording sensory responses. Nevertheless, if students are asked to rely upon firsthand observations but are not given clear directions on how to carry the assignment forward to its completion, they may feel lost. A form that helps them to gather, to record, and to organize data, therefore, can be especially helpful.

Since many firsthand reports require a clear separation of the processes of description, interpretation, and evaluation and since fuzzy thinking leads some students to make few distinctions among these processes, they may require clear explanation. To assume that the class knows well how to keep them apart in firsthand reporting is to court disappointment all the way around. Thus, in instructions for a paper based on observation, you may have to direct students to separate verifiable data from inferences and from judgments. Other kinds of writing, of course, require these distinctions; in firsthand observation, however, the instinct to merge the categories is especially strong.

To facilitate the recording of information, the instruction form often includes space for students to fill in both brief reactions as well as more extended analyses, if necessary. Comments recorded on the form also provide the data for the final report based on the observation and submitted for evaluation. Therefore, a review of the two preceding strategies on the brief writing assignment and the longer paper, respectively, might be helpful at this point. You have to stress clarity of content, editorial care, student accountability, and efficient pacing in the observation report just as you do in any guidelines for writing. And of course, a clear statement of the assignment is of prime importance here too.

The following steps should help you design a form that will elicit from students a report built on observations and including interpretations and judgments drawn from those observations. Sample forms building upon these steps appear in figures 8.2–8.5. One observation report form is for a museum report; the other is for a field visit to a community agency.

Strategy 8: Assigning Field and Laboratory Reports

Step 1: List the areas for which you expect students to record observations. It is not enough simply to tell your students to "observe"—especially if they are inexperienced with the discipline and have not yet developed a sense of what advanced students probably know without thinking: the categories that can help a researcher record and organize experience that otherwise may remain unfocused. Before you can provide instructions, you first must determine exactly the areas of information you want students to come away with based on observations you expect them to make. An art instructor* listed these pieces of information, for example, that he wanted included in a museum report:

- Visual elements used in the painting observed
- Depth techniques used by artist
- Design principles used by artist
- Subject matter of the observed painting

* All examples and materials from art in this strategy were adapted from the work of Peter Brown.

Step 2: Use cue words or question words to structure comments that will elicit from students the information you have listed. (For a full discussion of the uses of and the distinctions between cue words and question words, see pages 89–90.) Using as points of departure the areas of information defined above, the art instructor prepared these statements among others to guide students' recording of data:

> List in order of dominance at least four of the visual elements used in this painting. Then, in a brief sentence, tell specifically where in the painting the artist used them.

> Specifically describe the space of this painting. Identify and describe the dominant techniques used by the artist to show depth.

> List at least two dominant design principles used by this artist to organize and unify the painting.

> Identify the subject matter of this painting.

For a human services course on aging, an instructor* provided these guide statements for a visit to a health services center for senior citizens:

> Describe the physical appearance of the place you visited, including size, atmosphere, and numbers and kinds of rooms.

> List the various kinds of equipment or specialized machines you saw. Explain the purposes of at least two.

Step 3: Provide instructions about procedures, if necessary. Sometimes in order to carry out the observations properly, students need explanations about procedure. Here are parts of such sets of instructions:

> Note the travel directions, your expected arrival time, and the person to report to. If in doubt as to estimated travel time from your home, contact the Transit Authority for information. Allow additional time so that you arrive prior to the scheduled time.

> Follow the instructions of the tour leader.

> Bring pad, pencil, and this form; plan to spend approximately three hours.

> Obtain a museum pass from your instructor.

Step 4: If it is necessary for the assignment, clarify in writing the distinctions among description, interpretation, and evaluation. If the assignment involves students in describing, in interpreting, and then,

---

* All examples and materials from human services in this strategy were adapted from the work of Naomi Greenberg.

perhaps, in evaluating different experiences, you will need to distinguish among these activities. The report, whatever its basis, will no doubt require information rooted in varied thinking categories, and these will need to be clarified for students. *Description* is the record of events or objects as they appear to the observer's senses. *Interpretation* involves explanation and analysis in an effort to understand observations. *Evaluation* generally means making a judgment, either by offering a personal like or dislike or by asserting which of a limited field is best—or both—*and* by offering reasons for making the judgment. Often *interpretation* and *evaluation* cannot be easily separated. Yet if students are asked to make these distinctions, you will need to define and distinguish them from each other.

Just how you separate the categories will depend, of course, upon the assignment itself and the way it draws upon them. An art instructor offers students the following explanation in guidelines for a paper on a museum report:

> *Descriptive Analysis* requires you to use your own eyes to locate and to identify the formal, objective qualities of the painting, e.g., the visual elements and principles of design. Be sure to identify clearly the dominant elements and design principles by referring to specific subject matter and/or formal quality. For example: *focal point*—"The red roof of the house in the center functions as a focal point"; *line*—"My eye follows the line of the woman's arm to the right . . . there is a blue, diagonal line on the left side of the painting."

> *Interpretive Analysis* requires you to explain the subjective qualities of the painting: content and meaning. Interpretation means you must engage yourself to a "visual dialogue." Your response to this painting will be determined by both intrinsic criteria (subject matter, theme, mood) and extrinsic criteria (associations, memory, the opinions of others). Interpretive analysis involves both objective observation and open imagination. Be sure to make reference to specific qualities (descriptive analysis) to back up your interpretation of the meaning. For example: "The man in the center of this composition appears happy; the bright primary colors used throughout the painting create this impression . . . the basic theme of this painting is the joyous relationship of the man and the woman."

> *Evaluative Analysis* requires you to state opinions based on the form and content of the painting. Evaluative criticism asks that you judge this painting for artistic merit and explain your judgment. Is it a good painting? Why? Do you like it? Why?

Step 5: State clearly the requirements for any essay included in the assignment. For a discussion of how to phrase assignments, see Strategy 5.

Two museum visits for an art class culminated in the following essay assignment:

Directions for a Comparative Essay: You have completed an analysis of two paintings. Now write a three-page essay comparing these two paintings (*to compare* means "to give both similarities and differences"). Draw upon the distinctions made among *description, interpretation,* and *evaluation.* In your first paragraph, be sure to indicate the similarities and differences between the two paintings in terms of both form and content. Then, in the remainder of the essay, use specific facts and details to support your point.

A field report covering an agency for the aged included this assignment:

Write a two-page essay to present the program for a person who is considering the use of the agency's services but who has little knowledge about it. Use the responses you wrote directly on this handout as the basis for your report. In your introduction (a paragraph or two), name the agency and describe its most important physical features. Name the various funding sources, the sponsoring organization, and indicate whether the program is voluntary, government-supported, nonprofit, or proprietary.

In your next paragraph, identify the makeup of the clients/patients served by the program visited. (Consider the following areas: age, sex, and diagnoses.) Then list the variety of health professionals the program uses. In your next paragraphs, specify the service offered. In your conclusion (one or two paragraphs), *evaluate* the agency and make a recommendation to your reader as to whether or not the person should use its services.

Step 6: State clearly due dates, manuscript requirements, and proofreading responsibilities. Inclusion of such statements in the instructions you give for this report will help students complete the assignment in a timely, grammatical, and clear fashion. For example, the collection section of a museum report is shown in Figure 8.1, page 73.

Step 7: Create a handout for students. All the steps above should lead to the creation of a handout of instructions for students. The two examples provided in Figures 8.1 and 8.2—one for a report on a viewing in a museum and the other for a report on a field visit to a health agency—show, despite their necessary differences, careful attention to the concepts explored in this chapter.

Introduction to Art   Name _____

Museum Report   Date due _____

Museum Report: A comparison of two paintings in the Museum of
                 Modern Art, 53rd Street, between 5th and 6th
                 Avenues, E or F train to 5th Avenue.

Purpose: To compare two paintings from the Museum's
                 collection using vocabulary and critical ter-
                 minology and concepts that relate to the three
                 types of art criticism: descriptive, interpretive,
                 evaluative.

Procedures:

1.   Obtain a museum pass from your instructor.

2.   Visit the museum (museum hours listed on pass).

3.   Bring pad, pencil, and this form; plan to spend
     approximately three hours.

4.   Locate and look at all of the paintings paired in the
     list below.

5.   Then, choose one of these pairs to compare and contrast.
     All paintings are in galleries on the second floor.

     a.   G. deChirico, The Anxious Journey, Rm. 2
          H. Rousseau, The Dream, Rm. 2

     b.   P. Picasso, Three Musicians, Rm. 4
          P. Picasso, Three Women at the Spring, Rm. 5

     c.   P. Mondrian, Broadway Boogie Woogie, Rm. 8
          C. Monet, Waterlillies, Rm. 9

     d.   U. Boccioni, The City Rises, Rm. 10
          H. Matisse, The Piano Lesson, Rm. 11

     e.   E. Hopper, Gas, Rm. 16
          S. Davis, Lucky Strike, Rm. 16

     f.   R. Bearden, Patchwork Quilt, Rm. 16
          A. Wyeth, Cristina's World, Rm. 16

6.   Carefully observe the two paintings. Remember you do not
     have to "like" the paintings to complete the assignment.
     Begin to take notes based on your own observations; a final
     draft should be written on the assignment form later.

7. There are four sections to your report:
(a) descriptive analysis, (b) interpretive analysis,
(c) evaluative analysis, and (d) comparative essay.
Read each section carefully before taking notes.

I will check the following pieces of the assignment on
the dates indicated:

A. Descriptive Analysis:
Painting #1 _____   Painting #2 _____

B. Interpretive Analysis:
Painting #1 _____   Painting #2 _____

C. Evaluative Analysis:
Painting #2 _____   Painting #2 _____

D. Comparative Essay: _____

Figure 8.1 (continued)

To Guide Pacing:

Assignment due:_____

I will check the following pieces of
the assignment on the dates indicated:

Descriptive Analysis:
Painting #1 _____   Painting #2 _____

Interpretive Analysis:
Painting #1 _____   Painting #2 _____

Evaluative Analysis:
Painting #1 _____   Painting #2 _____

Comparative Essay: _____

To Encourage Careful Manuscript Form:

Begin to take notes on your own observations;
a final draft should be written on the assignment form later.

To Encourage Proofreading and Student Accountability:

Please read, complete, and sign the following
statement:

I have carefully read my assignment for my usual
errors in _____, _____, and
_____ and have corrected those mistakes
as best as I could. I went to the Writing Center
on _____ for special help.

_____
Signature

Figure 8.1 (continued)

<u>Gathering Data</u>

The following pages offer blank spaces for you to record your impressions of the paintings for three critical areas: <u>descriptive</u> analysis, <u>interpretive</u> analysis, and <u>evaluative</u> analysis. Use the explanations below to guide you as you write in your responses.

<u>Descriptive Analysis</u>: requires you to use your own eyes to locate and to identify the formal, objective qualities of the painting, e.g., the visual elements and principles of design. Be sure to identify clearly the dominant elements and design principles by referring to specific subject matter and/or formal quality.
For example: <u>focal point</u> -- "The red roof of the house in the center functions as a focal point"; <u>line</u> -- "My eye follows the line of the woman's arm to the right...there is a blue, diagonal line on the left side of the painting."

<u>Interpretive Analysis</u>: requires you to explain the subjective qualities of the painting: content and meaning. Interpretation means you must engage yourself in a "visual dialogue." Your response to this painting will be determined by both intrinsic criteria (subject matter, theme, mood) and extrinsic criteria (associations, memory, the opinions of others). Interpretive analysis involves both objective observation and open imagination. Be sure to make reference to specific qualities to back up your interpretation of the meaning. For example: "The man in the center of this composition appears happy; the bright primary colors used throughout the painting create this impression...the basic theme of this painting is the joyous relationship of the man and the woman."

<u>Evaluative Analysis</u>: requires you to state opinions based on form and content of the painting. Evaluative criticism asks that you judge this painting for artistic merit and explain your judgment. Is it a good painting? Why? Do you like it? Why?

Figure 8.1 (continued)

	Painting #1	Painting #2
	Artist _____	Artist _____
	Title _____	Title _____

A. Descriptive Analysis

1. List in order of dominance at least four of the visual elements used in this painting. Then, in a brief sentence, tell specifically where in the painting the artist used them.

   a.

   b.

   c.

   d.

   (Painting #2)

   a.

   b.

   c.

   d.

2. Specifically describe the space of this painting. Identify and describe the dominant techniques used by the artist to show depth.

Figure 8.1 (continued)

Painting #2
(continued)

a.

b.

Painting #1
(continued)

3.   List at least two   a.
dominant design
principles used by   b.
this artist to
organize and to
unify the painting.

4.   In the blank space
draw a diagram of the
line structure of this
painting. Locate the
focal point(s) with an
X. Use arrows to
indicate eye movement.
Below your diagram
briefly identify and
describe the relation
of subject matter to
linear structure (e.g.,
the red roof is the
focal point...the tree
is the dominant vertical...
a diagonal runs from the
girl in the lower right
to the horses in the
distance on the left).

Figure 8.1 (continued)

	Painting #1 (continued)	Painting #2 (continued)
B. Interpretive Analysis		
1. Identify the subject matter of the painting.		
2. Identify the principal theme (if any) and explain how the title of the painting helps to express this theme.		
3. Beyond subject matter and theme, explain and interpret any narrative content you see in this painting.		
4. Explain the content of this painting in terms of mood or feelings. Describe how the painting makes you feel. Use reference to specific formal qualities, e.g., "The dominance of dark blues, grays and blacks make this painting sad."		

Figure 8.1 (continued)

	Painting #1 (continued)	Painting #2 (continued)
C. Evaluative Analysis 1. Give your opinion about whether or not this painting is well executed, and whether or not the artist demonstrates appropriate technical skill. Explain your opinions.		
2. Explain whether or not this painting is aesthetically pleasing to you.		
3. Explain the significance (if any) which this painting holds for you.		

Figure 8.1 (continued)

D. <u>Directions for Comparative Essay</u>: Using the information from the previous pages, write a three-page essay comparing the two paintings you have just analyzed (to compare means "to show similarities and to contrast means to show differences"). Draw upon the distinctions made among <u>description</u>, <u>interpretation</u>, and <u>evaluation</u>. In your first paragraph, be sure to identify the similarities and differences between the two paintings in terms of both form and content. Then, in the remainder of the essay use specific facts and details to support your points. Use separate paper. <u>The essay you submit must be typed</u>. See General Writing Requirements in the course Learning Guide for specifics with regard to manuscript form.

Please read, complete, and sign the following statement, and submit it attached to your comparative essay.

    I have carefully read my assignment for my
    usual errors in _____, _____,
    and _____ and have corrected those
    mistakes as best as I could. I went to the
    Writing Center on _____ for Special
    help.

                              _____
                              Signature

Figure 8.1 (continued)

SCH 111 - AGING AS A HEALTH PROCESS

FIELD VISIT REPORT FORMAT

Instructions. For this assignment you will be required to visit a health program and to record your observations of it. Aside from general directions, this handout provides questions and spaces for you to write responses to those questions. Record information carefully: your answer will serve as the basis for your written report. Read this handout carefully the day of scheduled visit so that you know the kind of questions to ask.

Name _____

Date of Visit _____

Program Visited _____

Address _____

Name and Title of Staff Member Contacted _____

Objectives: To achieve visual awareness of a health program serving the aged. To observe the environmental conditions of that program. To differentiate between observation and evaluation when collecting data during a scheduled visit. To write a description and an evaluation of this health program.

Procedures: Study the travel directions, your expected arrival time and the person to report to. If in doubt as to estimated travel time from your home, contact the Transit Authority for information. Allow additional time to arrive prior to the scheduled time.

Consider the setting you are to visit when deciding how to dress for the day.

Take this handout with you as a guide sheet. Also take a pen or pencil and record information directly on the handout. You will write a report (see assignment below) based upon your notes.

Figure 8.2

Ask relevant questions (within the alloted time period) of the tour leader or others to whom you are introduced to help you clarify your observations.

Due Dates: Visit(s) to agency: _____
Completed report handout _____
Agency report: first draft _____
Agency report: final draft _____

A. <u>Description and Interpretation</u>

Your first effort is to observe and to record what you see and then to interpret it. <u>Description</u> requires that you rely upon sensory resources to identify the physical elements of the agency, its stated objectives, its clients, and so on. <u>Interpretation</u> requires that you explain your perception of what an agency or individual is attempting to accomplish. (You will have to ask questions of your tour leader in order to supplement your own observations.)

1. Describe the physical appearance of the place you visited, including size, atmosphere, and number and kinds of rooms.

2. List the types of employees available. Tell which ones worked together and describe how they related to each other. Describe at least two tasks that you observed them doing. Tell why the center employs some of these people.

3. Describe the kinds of people serviced at the health program by telling their ages, where some of them came from, and the reasons for their placement in the agency. Name some of the problems of these people. Explain how the agency attempts to deal with any of the problems you observed.

4. List the various kinds of equipment or specialized machines that you saw. Explain the purposes of at least two.

5. Describe any relevant printed materials that you noticed, such as a flyer, a newsletter or a brochure related to your observations, a posted certificate, or a calendar of activities. Explain the purpose of any one of them.

B. <u>Evaluation</u>

Now you must make some judgment about this agency. An <u>evaluation</u> requires that you offer your personal reactions to what you saw. And you must comment on those reactions occasionally by explaining <u>why</u> you feel as you do.

6. Give your first impressions as you entered the facility and moved through it. Tell whether or not you believe that the facility suits the clients it serves and why you believe as you do.

Figure 8.2 (continued)

7. Explain the difference between the population actually served and the population you expected to see. Give your opinion about any factors that would influence your decision to get services for a member of your family in this facility.

8. Give your personal reactions to the activities of one or two of the health professionals you observed.

9. State your opinion about whether or not the program was well organized. Explain your reasons, and indicate any changes you believe might be necessary.

10. State what impressed you most about the visit by explaining what you liked best and what you liked least about it.

C. Written Report

On separate paper, write a two-page essay to describe the program for a person who is considering using its services, but who has little knowledge about it. Use the responses you wrote to the questions above as the basis for your report. In your introduction (a paragraph or two), name the agency and describe its most important physical features. Name the various funding sources and the sponsoring organization, and indicate whether the program is voluntary, government-supported, nonprofit, or proprietary.

In your next paragraphs, identify the makeup of the clients/patients served by the program visited. (Consider the following areas: age, sex, and diagnoses.) Then list the variety of health professionals the program uses. In your next paragraphs, specify the services offered. In your conclusion (one or two paragraphs), evaluate the agency and make a recommendation to your reader as to whether or not the person you plan to advise should use its services.

On the due date indicated, you will read rough drafts in groups and will discuss with group members the strengths and weaknesses of individual reports.

Final drafts must be typed and must follow guidelines for manuscript preparation.

Figure 8.2 (continued)

Part III

Strategies for Encouraging Students' Effective Use of Oral and Listening Skills in Content Courses

9 | Structuring Questions to Foster Purposeful Listening and Discussion

Overview

Human conversation can be a most satisfying activity, providing us with the information and insights we need to carry on our lives. It can also, of course, be a most frustrating activity when the give and take of conversation stops and "bilateral" monologue begins. Nothing, perhaps, is more vexing than the conversation in which our questions or statements are either not "heard" or are misunderstood, in which, like Prufrock, we confront a disappointed listener who shakes his head and says: "That is not what I meant at all. That is not it, at all."

The opportunities for conversation surround us. The classroom, however, presents an opportunity for a particularly concentrated conversation. In the average class, some sort of interaction—whether it is student to student, student to teacher, teacher to student, or a combination of these—is central to the learning process and often accounts for the major portion of class time. Classroom interaction, as we all know, can be a most exhilarating experience as students attain and demonstrate new knowledge and understanding, but it can also be downright demoralizing.

We have all stood painfully before classes that struggle to respond to a question, a question that we are certain is easy and direct. Perhaps no one in the class raises a hand to answer, and we feel compelled to state the question in alternative forms once, twice, even three times. Perhaps students respond but do not address the question we thought we asked; or perhaps they do not supply the information we expected the question to elicit, and we have to repeat and rephrase the response so it allows the line of thought to proceed. Perhaps students offer only a yes-or-no response to our question or provide only a word or two to address an issue we expected to stimulate a more complex answer. Is the problem that students do not really listen and identify what is being asked of them, or is it that they have difficulty phrasing the kind of response we expect? Probably it is a little of both. Discussion, after all, depends not only on focused listening but on focused responding as well, and the lack of student focus on either area will cause discussion to lag. Sometimes, too, we may be the problem: the way we structure our questions may not foster either effective listening or effective responses in the classroom.

Carefully planned discussion, however, can often help students listen and respond meaningfully. During the course of an hour, a barrage of information and ideas flies through the room, and the most well-intentioned students may struggle to pay attention to everything. If we do not help the class organize and sort out the heaps of information, a kind of lopsided listening can result in which the student enlarges smaller points and diminishes larger ones.

Many techniques can help you improve class discussion. By presenting at the start of each class the critical questions that the class discussion or lecture will "answer," we have one method of helping students to locate just what in all that is said is worth attending to. Then, too, how we phrase ongoing questions can help focus students' inquiry and responses. A poorly phrased question can frustrate students' efforts in responding during discussion: a rising voice at the end of a sentence does not guarantee that we are asking an answerable question. Certainly, each of us can remember situations in which a question of ours that we thought perfectly clear floundered while different students tried in vain to keep it afloat—and while we shook our head or said, "Anyone else know what I'm looking for?" Language that makes our questions clear—an example, a reason, an interpretation, perhaps—can guide students toward satisfying responses.

The following strategy will (a) present steps to help you develop "focus questions," questions shared with students in advance of instruction to guide listening, as well as (b) present steps to help you develop ongoing questions to structure and direct student responses as the class proceeds.

Good discussion builds one upon the other—careful listening and purposeful responding, attentive and thoughtful reception and transmission of information and ideas.

Strategy 9: Structuring Questions to Foster Purposeful Listening and Discussion

Step 1: Review the language and format of questions. Whatever use we make of questions in the classroom—to focus listening or to direct responses—the way we structure the question, the words and syntax we use, can be important, helping or hindering us in our purpose.

Let us consider some different styles of questions. A very basic distinction involves the differences between the "open" and the "closed" question. Open questions are broad, allowing a respondent a wide range of answers. Questions such as "What can you tell us about the war?" or "What do you think are the major causes of the war?" or "Why do you think the peace efforts failed?" are all open because respondents define the terms of their responses. The second and third questions, though still considered open questions, limit and direct responses more than the first question does. Open questions can vary in the extent of their openness, yet all allow a range of freedom for the respondent. In general, open questions tend to establish a sense of rapport and inquiry. The wide-open question, however, runs the risk of letting the answerer roam free and possibly get lost.

The closed question narrows the answerer's range of possible responses. Questions such as "Do you believe the war was just?" or "Whom do you think was hurt most—the North or the South?" are closed questions because they demand a rather precise focus. Although such closed questions are useful for getting students to see where they stand on a particular issue, they risk stifling further exploration and analysis of a topic. Hence they should be used judiciously.

In structuring questions, whether open or closed, we should be aware of the meaning of the words most commonly used in questions—*how, why, what, which, where, when, who*. Each question word makes a particular demand on potential respondents. For the most part, what is requested by the question words *who, which, when*, and *where* is usually clear. But *why, how*, and (at times) *what* are not quite as obvious in their requirements. The word *why*, for example, can take respondents into a misty region where we may or may not have intended them to go. In a social science course, we may ask students *why* they supported a particular candidate. One student might say that he met the candidate on the street and trusted his eyes; another might describe the candidate's attributes; another might indicate how listening to the candidate speak made her feel hopeful about the future of cities. In a sense, all these answers answer the question *why*. Yet more often than not, when we ask *why* in the classroom, we expect a particular line of reasoning—one that reflects modes of thought in our discipline—to follow. If in fact we do have a particular approach in mind, the language of our questions must show it. If the teacher who asks the question about the presidential candidate wants responses along *one* of the lines presented by students and not all, he or she must follow his or her *why* question with a "directive" that leads the student where he or she wants: "Why did you support X as a candidate? Try to describe those attributes that led you to choose him."

In constructing follow-up directives, it is helpful to make use of "cue words," words that guide students in a specific way. Such words specify the particular mental operations you wish students to undertake and thereby offer clear guidance. Some of these cue words and their definitions were presented in Strategy 5. That list, however, is not exhaustive, nor are the definitions "definitive." As was noted, the needs of your discipline, your course, and your students might suggest refinements to these definitions and/or other words—*infer, summarize, estimate, justify, evaluate*, etc.

For the clear-cut question words (*who, when, where, which*, and *what* at times), you probably will not need to follow up with directives built on cue words. However, it is interesting to note that some cue words and some question words can elicit the same responses:

- Who is called the "Father of the Impressionists"?
- Which war was called "the war to end all wars"?
- When did Langston Hughes write his autobiography?
- Where did Francis Bacon get his ideas on rhetoric?
- What are the characteristics of the "borderline" personality?

- Name the person called the "Father of the Impressionists."
- Identify the "war to end all wars."
- State the date of Langston Hughes's autobiography.
- Identify the sources of Francis Bacon's ideas on rhetoric.
- Identify the characteristics of the "borderline" personality.

Yet a quick reading aloud of the above items should make it clear that while a question and a directive may yield a similar response, it is probably preferable to use the question word in an oral situation. For the question word establishes a greater sense of communication and inquiry and is thus more conducive and more appropriate to oral interaction than is the cue word. The latter, on the other hand, gives a command rather than asks a question, and this syntactic and grammatical imperative can create an odd, imperious ring in the classroom.

In summary, although the question words *who*, *which*, *when*, and *where* are fairly explicit in the kinds of tasks they suggest, *how*, *why*, and *what* are not quite so clear-cut. Sometimes in class you may want the wide range of responses that certain question words establish. In order to encourage varied perspectives on an issue, you may want different students to perform different mental operations implied by a broad question. Sometimes, however, you might want a very focused answer—a description, perhaps, or a precise example. Yet if you use only open-ended question words to get at the description, you might be disappointed. Therefore, decide what sorts of answers you want, and use language and constructions that will move the class where you want it to go.

Such clear questions, as we have suggested, are apt to yield fruitful results not only in spoken responses during class discussion but also as students listen to material in silence.

Step 2: Create "focus questions" to guide students' listening, and present them at the start of the class. With some of the styles and language of questioning in mind, you can turn to specific applications of questions in the classroom. As indicated earlier, one useful time to use questions is at the beginning of a class. It is true that when a class session begins, students generally have some idea of the topic to be covered. But if students also have a mental framework to hold together the information we present, they will be better able to remember just what it is we have said. They will be better able to deal with the information—to apply it, to analyze and synthesize it, to assess it. Without such a mental framework, however, we may well find students recalling only disconnected pieces of information, thus not taking in the basic knowledge required for advanced thinking in the discipline.

Giving students "focus questions" in advance of instruction is an effective way to clue students in not only to the sequence of topics we will cover but also to the level of thinking that we expect about the topic. Many of us do something like this already: we begin a class lecture or discussion with a brief overview of topics to be covered. But using questions to provide this initial organization is particularly effective, for questions activate students' minds, encouraging problem solving and inquiry in a way that the mere announcing of topics cannot. Transforming important topics at the start into "focus questions" encourages purposeful, focused listening and thinking about the topic. Telling students in an art class, for example, that the class discussion for the day will attempt to answer two questions—"*What* are the distinctive thematic and stylistic features of Van Gogh's and Gauguin's paintings?" and "*How* do the two artists compare in terms of these features?"—is far more stimulating than merely saying, "Today we will consider Gauguin and Van Gogh."

Using cue words to develop directives can also be effective for providing an initial focus for class discussion. Such directives organize the class discussion around a few important tasks. The art class considered above, for example, could be told that the class that day will first analyze the thematic and stylistic features of Van Gogh's and Gauguin's painting and then compare the work of the two artists.

Both focus questions and directives can be used effectively at the start of the class to focus listening and subsequent discussion. Which format you decide on will depend somewhat on your individual style and the means you choose for getting these focusing guides to your students. If you present them aloud, you may be more comfortable stating them as questions in order to maintain a more conversational tone. If, however, you present your foci for discussion in writing—on the board or in a handout—directives may feel just as comfortable as questions to you and your students.

In order to practice developing "focus questions" (or directives), you will want to follow a few steps. (a) Begin by looking at the materials you use to deliver the *first* content lesson you teach. These materials may be in the form of notes, outlines, or perhaps a marked-up script. (b) From these materials, check off the main points for which you will hold students accountable. (c) Jot down just what you expect students to do with these points in the course of the lesson—comprehend, apply, analyze, synthesize, evaluate, and so on. (d) With these mental operations in mind, transform each point into a "focus question" (or a directive). As an example, look at some of the focusing directives* developed for a lecture in a film course:

---

* Adapted from the work of Joyce Rheuban.

- Define the concept *cinematic*.
- Define what is a "good" and what is a "bad" film.
- Compare the presentation of an action, incident, or story on stage and a presentation of the same action, incident, or story on film.
- Define the word *aesthetic*.
- Define the word *artistic*.
- Explain the difference between watching a film subjectively and watching a film objectively.

(e) Once you have developed a set of questions to focus students' attention for a particular lesson, decide how you will present them to students—on paper as a handout distributed for consideration at the end of the previous lesson, on the board for consideration at the start of a lesson, out loud as the class begins. (f) Finally, once you have created the questions you will use to focus students' listening in the first session in which you present content, you will want to review these questions to be sure they are as focused as possible. Focus questions that set the scope for an entire lesson tend to be more open than the questions that arise along the way in class discussion. Therefore, you will want to ask yourself certain questions. Do any of the questions you wrote use an open format when you expect a much more restricted reply? Are *how* and *why* questions followed, where necessary, by directives using specific cue words to focus a reply? Are there questions written to cover all the major topics? Do the questions you wrote cue students in to the level of thinking about the topics you expect, or do they suggest that mere recall will be enough when other operations—analysis and application, let us say— are key to grasping the material?

Using "focus questions" and focusing directives to alert students to your expectations will help them know what to listen for and, in turn, will form the basis for successful classroom interaction.

Step 3: Create questions to focus ongoing discussion. Good discussion, as we have been stressing above, depends not only on good listening but also on purposeful and focused responses. In the classroom, once you have laid out for focus the major "questions" that the class will attempt to answer or the major tasks to be performed in a particular session, you will want to develop questions (or directives) to use along the way to guide students' responses. Unlike the "focus questions" considered above, these questions are not intended as "advance organizers" of information and ideas but rather as "on-the-spot" guides. Again, it will probably be helpful to develop these questions out of the materials you use to teach. To gain practice in doing this, (a) again review the materials—notes, outlines, script, etc.—from which you teach the *first* content lesson of your course and (b) indicate the points you want students to grasp. (c) Then develop a question for each of these points. For the sake of economy and efficiency, you may want to write these questions in the margin of your regular teaching materials.

Obviously, the teaching act cannot be completely planned out. Good teaching is interactive, and you will, out of necessity, find yourself posing questions on the spur of the moment. The objective here is not to stifle spontaneity—creating questions on the spur of the moment during your class session is important too—but to locate strategic places to insert well-structured questions and directives.

The approaches considered above—the creation of focus questions and the creation of ongoing classroom questions—should help you to help your students make better use of the discussion process—listening, thinking, and responding with purpose. Of course, this section has only begun to touch on the uses of questions in the classroom. Their value cannot be overestimated. Beyond the applications mentioned, we can use questions as checks on students' perceptions, as pointers to new contexts, as probes to deepen discussion. Probes such as "What do you have in mind?" "Why do you think that's so?" for example, can be used effectively to push students to think and respond more deeply, and such probes will be discussed in Strategy 9, where we deal with ways to help students focus their responses.

Step 4: Tape a class and evaluate the effectiveness of your questions in focusing listening and responding. Arrange to audiotape (or, better yet, videotape) at least one if not two or three content-oriented class sessions. (a) Then review the focus questions and statements you distributed (or announced) in advance of instruction. (b) Listen to the tape, and make a list of the questions you posed throughout the session, being sure to capture the exact language of each question and of any follow-up directives using cue words. (c) Then evaluate your effectiveness. Draw conclusions about the types of questions you prepared on the spot. Also note the types of responses students gave when you used specific question words and specific cue words. Did you use certain words that did not produce the intended results? If so, you may have to tell students early in the course their responsibilities in classroom discussions and to explain and to illustrate the types of responses you expect when you use specific question words and specific cue words. Such a statement could easily be included as part of a more general learning guide (see Strategy 15 for ways to develop such a guide and for examples).

As you review your list of questions, you will find it helpful to review them against a checklist of unproductive questions and questioning techniques. The beginnings of such a checklist appear below. You probably will want to add to the list after reflecting upon those questions you have heard others using or, inadvertently, have used yourself.

| *Polite Questions* | Can you compare capitalism and communism? | Although the asker of this question expects more than affirmation, respondents can fail to recognize the implications |

		of the questions and their colloquially polite structures.
Catch-All Questions	*How about* the relationship of fashion to culture? (or) *What about* the rise of nationalism in pre-World War I Germany?	Respondents can say almost anything they wish though the teacher may have something quite specific in mind.
Tag-On Questions	Why does the poet use the word *chariot* instead of *cart*? Then, what connotations does the word *chariot* have? What does a chariot mean to you?	The respondent cannot concentrate on any one question long enough to formulate a response because each question is quickly followed by another. Though the questioner may believe she or he is clarifying the initial question by restating it, she or he is, in fact, creating new questions that require different responses.

Often, when teachers listen to or watch class interaction on tape, they are quite pleased at what they find. Questions are focused; responses are direct and to the point. Yet generally, they are surprised by some of the observations they make.

Taping your classes can help you determine specific ways in which you can more clearly phrase your questions. Taping a few consecutive sessions will enable you to capture the "real you" and to identify steps in your questioning techniques as well as problems common to your students' response styles. Awareness of such patterns will enable you and your students to use discussion more effectively for grasping and confirming learning.

10 | Developing Oral Assignments

Overview

Rhetoric, the art of speech making, is perhaps the most time-honored subject in Western education, dating back to fifth-century Greece and stretching forward to the past century. A hundred years ago school children still studied the classical techniques of persuasive discourse, and graduation from academies and colleges often depended on an ability to speak before an audience with convincing arguments and lively language. Though both the study and the practice of formal rhetoric in our schools have declined considerably, the need remains to practice and perfect skills in sustained oral discourse. Perhaps we no longer see the sense in requiring students to develop skills in the classical rhetorical areas and topics—in deliberative, forensic, and epideictic oratory, in speeches of praise or blame, on the expedient or inexpedient, on justice or injustice. Still, few of us would deny that the need for skill in oral discourse remains central not only to our personal lives but to our educational and professional lives as well. Certainly in advanced studies students must perform skillfully in such oral activities as seminar reports and oral examinations. In professional situations the need is steady—the oral case presentation of the physician, the psychologist, and the social worker; the oral report of the accountant, the administrator; the persuasive presentations of the community leader, the salesperson, and the lawyer all come to mind. Indeed, it is difficult to think of a profession that does not require from its practitioners some sort of sustained oral communication.

In the classroom students need to practice those skills in oral discourse that future educational and professional situations will demand. Students also need to use those skills in the courses they are currently taking in order to think through and share ideas aloud. Again and again in our classes we ask students to go beyond the "give and take" of discussion to some sustained oral assignment that allows the speaker to organize, to apply, and to demonstrate specialized knowledge and understandings.

Though many of us think of "speeches" when we think of oral assignments in the classroom, the truth is that oral assignments need not be, and generally are not, such formal undertakings. Oral assignments can be long or brief, formal or informal, depending on the demands of the course. A common oral activity has students apply knowledge and analytical skills acquired in the course to a new situation. In an art course, for example, teachers,* having defined the formal features of a painting, may ask students one by one, over a stretch of time, to review other paintings aloud. Usually, students will be asked to identify these features and to explain how they function in each piece. A math instructor,† after covering a particular principle, may give students individual problems and ask students to talk through an application of the principle. Indeed, the occasions for such activities present themselves in almost any class, and the benefits are numerous. Both the presenting student and the teacher are made aware of what the student knows or does not know, and the student audience can follow an entire logical sequence, filling in the pieces of information and operations about which they may have had doubts, checking their peers' thinking, checking their own.

Another common type of oral assignment, of course, is the more traditional formal presentation, in which students present aloud research findings from the library, the laboratory, or the field. Such an assignment may be the sole product of such a research effort, or it may be one of several products—an oral report, for example, highlighting material from an extended paper that the student has written. Oral assignments can be linked with research and writing tasks at some earlier stage as well. Students who have done some exploratory work on a topic may present preliminary findings and thoughts to the class in the expectation of discovering both dead ends and clear paths. Thus such an assignment can help the student gain control of material that he or she will later develop in written form.

The activities described above are just a few of the kinds of oral assignments found commonly in the classroom. The oral assignment, however, is an adaptable and versatile form, and the particular activity you choose to develop depends on your goals. The benefits of asking students to talk aloud about their knowledge and understandings are many, guiding students through important processes and toward satisfying products. Then, too, such activities provide presenting students with quick feedback on their work and the student audience with quick access to another person's thinking. In all classroom oral assignments— whether the presenters are applying a set of principles or operations to a new situation, formally presenting research, or exploring aloud approaches to an assignment in progress—the teaching activity is extended beyond the teacher, with students learning to assume responsibility for not just the reception but also for the development and transmission of ideas.

The steps in the following strategy will help you determine where learning in your course can be facilitated by oral assignments. Whatever oral assignments you may include in your courses, however, you need

* Peter Brown and Marguerita Grecco.
† Howard Kellogg.

to present clear guidelines that alert students to the steps involved. Helping students carefully plan these activities will help relieve them of the considerable anxiety that comes from facing the unknown. This strategy, then, will also help you create the guidelines that will make the process known to students and foster confidence and success in completing oral assignments from which they and others can learn.

Strategy 10: Developing Oral Assignments

Step 1: Decide when in your course oral assignments can be used to facilitate learning. The exact purpose and nature of the oral activities you use will depend upon your discipline, your course, your assessment of students' skills, even your teaching style. Before structuring any oral assignment, however, the first thing to determine is the point(s) in the course when sustained oral discourse of some sort—be it a brief application of principles to a new situation, a report based on field or lab observation, a formal presentation building on library research—can help students think through and arrive at understandings. To identify these points, you will need to review both your course syllabus and the course notes from which you teach, while asking yourself questions such as the following: Are there operations or principles that students are taught and then are expected to apply? At what points in the syllabus is the teaching of an operation or principle completed? Would an oral assignment in which students describe and analyze a new application help to facilitate learning? Is there a research assignment in the field, library, or laboratory that would effectively culminate in or benefit from an oral presentation? Is there a writing or research assignment that would benefit from students' talking aloud about their plans and progress? As you answer these questions, check off on the syllabus just where you think it would be helpful to assign an oral presentation and just what kind of assignment that might be.

Only after you have determined when and what type of oral assignments to require can you think about structuring the assignments. This involves developing a statement of the central task for each assignment as well as developing additional guidelines to help students accomplish the task. For each of the points in your syllabus where you have decided that an oral assignment would work, you will need to do these things. The process is laid out in the steps below.

Step 2: Word the task clearly. In developing oral assignments, just as in developing writing assignments, you must word clearly the central task that students are to perform. Follow the directions laid out in Strategy 5: (a) select specific cue words to focus the assignment, and develop a statement that identifies exactly what you want from students; (b) add any needed explanation of the cue words; (c) revise your statement of the task to eliminate ambiguities; and (d) require that students develop a statement of purpose and use it early in the presentation. (This last step will ensure that both the speaker and the audience can follow the direction of the presentation.) In addition, for the formal oral presentation, you will (e) want to indicate the length of the assignment in terms of the *maximum* time limit. A maximum is important because the general tendency of inexperienced speakers is to ramble, and you want to emphasize that students should be direct and to the point.

Here are some sample assignments for three kinds of oral activities. Note how each builds on a central task and also incorporates other explanations and directives.

> *Application of a Principle*: To gain skill in mathematics, it is important that you be aware of how you do what you do—how you solve problems, draw conclusions, prove theories, carry out algorithms, and so on. Since in this course we will be focusing primarily on solving problems, I will ask two students at each class meeting to *explain* how they arrived at a solution to a specific problem.*

> *Oral Report Based on Written Assignment*: In your written report on a chemical element you included such information as the source of the element in nature, methods of extraction and purification, properties of the element, common chemistry, and practical uses in everyday life. Using this written assignment as a basis, develop a five-minute oral presentation in which you *identify* and *explain* those areas of information that you find to be particularly interesting or enlightening. One of your first statements should clearly indicate which areas you will discuss and why. This statement is called, in writing assignments, a topic sentence, and in oral assignments, a statement of purpose.†

> *Observation Report*: After making a field visit to an assigned human services agency and completing in writing the Field Visit Report, you are to make a five-minute oral presentation to the class, based on your observation of the agency and your discussion with the staff there. In your presentation, you should *describe* the physical surroundings of the agency, *identify* the source of its funding, *explain* the agency's functions, and explain any conflict in interest due to funding requirements.‡

> *Oral Presentation Based on Research*: In a ten-minute (maximum) presentation, *explain* what you find interesting about some artist. The artist must be one whose work is of a particular interest to you and one who is noted in your text but not covered in class. (Be sure

---

* Adapted from the work of Howard Kellogg.
† Adapted from the work of Mary Lee Abkemeier.
‡ Adapted from the work of Betty Farber.

your presentation does not merely identify points of interest but also gives the reasons why these points are interesting.) In the first minute or two, state clearly the points about the artist that you will cover. Then, drawing upon your research, use specific factual details to develop your points.*

Step 3: Develop a set of guidelines that will let students know your expectations and help them pace their work. When faced with an oral assignment, students generally experience considerable anxiety, but careful planning on our part can help to reduce it. More often than not, anxiety in the classroom comes when students are unclear about the task at hand and do not understand fully the steps leading to the completion of the assignment.

Obviously, the steps students should follow in an oral assignment will be determined by the type of presentation you require. For a formal oral presentation, many of those steps will be the same as the steps involved in preparing a long writing assignment (see Strategy 7). But the oral task requires other steps as well, such as developing "cue cards" to speak from and "proofing" the presentation, on tape, perhaps. For a more informal oral assignment, of course, the steps involved will be fewer and less detailed than those involved in the formal task.

Your assignment, depending on its length and formality, may not follow *all* the steps discussed below, but it will certainly follow some. As you review each item, note that for formal oral presentations, these steps are ultimately incorporated, along with a timetable where appropriate, into a handout. (A sample handout appears in Figure 10.4.) These guidelines can, of course, be included in a learning guide prepared for students; however, for the more brief oral assignments, you may choose to offer the guidelines orally.

a. *Selecting a topic.* In order to be most helpful to students, you will want to guide them as they choose topics for oral presentations. Hence you might specify a single topic or a core of topics, or you might stipulate your wish to approve the students' individual choice of topic. In the sample assignment from an art class (pages 107–109), for example, note that the instructor asks students to limit their selection of topics not only to an artist who is covered in the text but also to one who does not appear in the syllabus and hence will not be covered in class. For the short informal assignment, especially one that asks students to apply some principle in a new context, you may want to influence the choice of that context—the particular painting, the poem, the mathematical problem, or the like. (See, for example, the art and math assignments described in the overview of this strategy.)

* Adapted from the work of Marguerita Grecco.

b. *Covering important areas.* Develop instructions that explain the areas and the issues that students should cover. For the informal assignment, this may involve no more than reviewing the principles or operations that you expect students to apply to a new context. For example, an English teacher may want to review with students those formal features of poetry that they are to include in their oral analyses. In preparation for an oral field report, the cooperative education instructor may want to identify for students the exact nature of the observations they must make at the industrial sites they visit. The teacher assigning library research may want to specify the issues to which the research should attend. Whatever the approach, the important thing is that you clarify with students the areas and issues you expect the presentation to cover.

c. *Doing library research.* If you require extended library research for the assignment, you will need to review research procedures for students, as you did for the long research assignment in writing (see Strategy 7).

d. *Taking focused notes and recording sources.* You also will need to make clear how you expect students to record relevant information. This may mean no more than reminding students to review key principles or operations that you have already shared with them and also to jot down how each of these applies to the new context they are considering. For the field or laboratory assignment, it may mean asking students to record relevant data on a specific form that you have developed. In this case, you will need to explain how to take notes using the form. If students will be doing library research, you will need to explain, perhaps by example, how to take focused notes as they read and how accurately to record bibliographic information as they proceed.

e. *Limiting the topic and developing a statement of purpose.* When students do not know what they want to say, they can waste hours recording information ultimately of little or no use to their assignment. Hence you will want to encourage class members to limit a topic by developing a statement of purpose as early as possible. That statement can be purely informational: "I have selected the poem 'Little Black Boy' and will be looking at the irony, imagery, and point of view in the work." It can be a statement of opinion: "I will show why *A Clockwork Orange* is a failed masterpiece." It can be persuasive: "I will try to convince you that Piaget's approach and not Skinner's is more successful in today's urban preschools." For reports on research, of course, students will need to preview sources before formulating their purpose statements. In order to assure both you and the student that he or she is on the right track, has a manageable topic, and has a fair chance of succeeding, you also may find it helpful to suggest that each student meet with you, by a specified time, to review both the topic and the purpose statement (see page 108). Obviously, this probably will not be necessary for the very brief oral presentation.

f. *Developing "cue cards."* Once students have collected all the necessary information, they will need to reorder their notes as cues from which to talk. This is true even for the briefest of oral assignments. In preparing a guideline to suggest how students should develop cue cards, it is important to stress the value of using written *phrases* rather than complete sentences or paragraphs. Approach head-on the instinct to write out speeches fully. Explain the problem that generally results from following that procedure: although it is true that some effective speakers can speak effectively from an edited manuscript, the edited manuscript presentation is an extremely difficult undertaking, relying on exceptionally good writing and effective oral skills. Few people can successfully make such a presentation. What generally happens in the classroom is that as the pressure mounts, students panic and then end up reading their papers and boring their audience.

If the goals are to have students gain experience and learn something about the topic while presenting ideas aloud and to have the audience learn something as well, the edited manuscript presentation generally will not prove effective. Hence, once students have taken and pulled together their notes, they should be encouraged to develop a set of "cue cards" which at the top have a very clear statement of purpose and to which every subsequent piece of information introduced is related.

g. *Practicing and "proofing" the presentation.* Merely suggesting that students practice their presentations rarely yields the intended results. Too often students assume that because they have recorded the necessary information on paper, they do not need to practice a presentation aloud. They assume that everything will come together when they stand before the group, but the result of an unpracticed speech is often like the first draft of a paper submitted without necessary editing and reworking.

Yet if students practice aloud, strong phrases do tend to stand out and inconsistencies do rise to the surface. For the brief assignment, all that may be needed is a single rehearsal. For the longer assignment, however, students should practice several times and should try to discover problems in their presentation before presenting it formally.

One way to encourage careful practice is to develop a set of guidelines that ask students (1) to practice their presentation *orally*, using cue cards. For the longer assignment, you might also ask students (2) to record their talks on tape and (3) to evaluate their own presentations using whatever principles of assessment you have developed. If you use a form for assessment (see sample in Figure 10.1), students can use a similar form for a preassessment (see Figure 10.2 for sample) of their own work and can hand the form in before or at the time of the presentation. Even the brief, informal talk will benefit from a little practice and "proof."

Step 4: Develop a method for recording your comments about students' presentations and for making clear how you and the class will share those comments with the speaker. Often teachers who are inexperienced in listening to formal oral reports assume that they can take a few general notes as students speak and can then offer comments off the cuff when the talk ends. Perhaps this practice works for the very brief assignment, but it generally will not work for an assignment of any length. Without a scheme for consistent evaluation, you are bound to overlook some features of some students' presentation, and with shifting grounds for judgment, you may grade unfairly. Hence it is important for longer assignments that you develop a method for recording your comments as each student speaks, being sure to comment on such areas as content, form, bibliography, cue cards, and perhaps, too, response to questions. You should also develop some system so that students can easily determine how you arrived at your grade. (You might find it helpful to bring carbon to class so that as you take notes, you can automatically create a copy for students.) Once you have created a form to give students feedback on their presentation, you should prepare a statement which describes the form and explains how you will use it to share your assessment with them. If the class will be permitted to ask questions, you should make this clear to students along with whether or not their ability to respond to questions will be included in your evaluation. Then, too, if the class in general will be asked to assess the presentation, you will want to indicate this and provide a form to facilitate peer feedback. Again, these methods relate to the longer, more formal assignment; for the shorter assignment, your informal comments will probably do the trick.

The forms in Figures 10.1–10.3 for teacher, peer, and self-assessment should serve as examples as you develop a format of your own for evaluating the longer oral presentation. (Sample guidelines for an oral presentation are given too; see Figure 10.4.)

Teacher Feedback Form

Student:_____
Date: _____

Content-Related Oral Communication Skills: I will consider here such things as statement of purpose, accuracy, and amount of information to support your proposal, sources cited aloud, particularly good information.

Possible points: 40   Points given:

_____

Form-Related Oral Skills: I will consider here such things as organization, fluency (or use of verbal fillers), your pronunciation, volume, pace, grammar, and style--including whether you talked from notes or were "manuscript sounding."

Possible points: 30   Points given:

_____

Cue Cards, Bibliography: I will consider here such things as relationship of what is on the cards and what was said; thoroughness in approach; number of secondary sources; correct bibliographic form.

Possible points: 20   Points given:

_____

Self-Analysis and Answers to Questions: I will comment here on the thoroughness of your self-analysis based on the self-analysis you submit, your ability to address anticipated questions, the content and form of your responses to questions.

Possible Points: 10   Points given:

_____

90-100   A   Total points: _____
80-89   B
70-79   C
65-69   D
Below 65 F   Grade: _____

Other Comments:

Figure 10.1

<u>Student Self-Assessment Form</u>

Student:_____

<u>Directions:</u>   Date: _____

1. Indicate below both the title of your presentation and
    your statement of purpose.

2. Practice your presentation aloud several times, being
    sure that all that you say adds to your purpose
    statement. When you feel good about how your presen-
    tation sounds, practice it aloud one more time but this
    time do it on tape.

3. Using the self-assessment form that follows, a form
    similar to the one I will use when I grade your report,
    listen to your tape and "proof" your presentation,
    taking notes on what aspects of its form or content
    still need work. Be sure that your comments focus
    on "problems" which still need to be addressed. Then
    assign yourself points for "content" and "form."

4. Next, review your cue cards and bibliographic
    information. Then record your assessment and indicate
    the points you would assign for these materials.

5. Finally, make a list of possible questions your class-
    mates or I may ask after you have given your
    presentation. Use the recorder again and tape your
    responses, jot down any problems, and again assign
    yourself points.

6. Add up the points in each category, and write in the
    total in the space provided.

7. Under "other comments," indicate your general perception
    of how you did and any thoughts you might have regarding
    the grade you expect.

Presentation Title: _____

    Statement of Purpose: _____

_____

_____

Figure 10.2

Content-Related Oral Communication Skills:
Comment here on any <u>problems</u> you see in terms of your
statement of purpose, accuracy and amount of information
to support the proposal, sources cited aloud, particularly
good information.

Possible points: 40   Points I would give myself:
_____

Form-Related Oral Skills: Comment here on any problems you see
in terms of organization, fluency (or use of verbal fillers),
pronunciation, volume, pace, grammar, style--including whether
presentation is "manuscript sounding."

Possible points: 30   Points I would give myself:
_____

Cue Cards and Bibliography: Comment here on any problems you
see in terms of the relationship of what is on cards to what
was said, thoroughness in approach, number of secondary
sources, correct form.

Possible points: 20   Points I would give myself:
_____

Questions I Anticipated Being Asked: List below questions which
you think either your classmates or I may ask once we hear your
presentation. Then answer them on tape and record any problems
you hear in terms of the content or form of your responses.
   List questions:

Indicate your assessment of your responses:

Possible points: 10   Points I would give myself:
_____
Assessment:
           90-100   A   Total Points: _____
           80-89   B
           70-79   C   Grade you would assign: _____
           65-69   D
           Below 65 F

Other comments:

Figure 10.2 (continued)

<u>Peer Feedback Form</u>

Title of Presentation: _____

Statement of Purpose (record as stated):

Content:

    1. List the points the speaker effectively
        covered.

    2. List the points you think needed more coverage.

Form (organization, fluency--or use of verbal fillers,
    volume, pace, grammar, style--including whether
    the person talks from notes or is "manuscript
    sounding"):

    3. Which oral communication behaviors did the
        speaker use well?

    4. Which oral communication behaviors need more
        attention (verbal fillers, volume, etc.)?

Figure 10.3

SAMPLE GUIDELINES

FOR AN ORAL PRESENTATION BASED ON RESEARCH

I. Assignment

In a ten-minute (maximum) presentation explain what you find interesting about an artist whose work is of particular interest to you, who is noted in your text but who is not covered in class. (Be sure your presentation does not merely identify points of interest but also gives the reasons why these points are interesting.) In the first minute or two state clearly the points about the artist that you will cover. Then drawing upon your research, use specific factual details to develop your points.

II. Procedures

A. Selecting a Topic

Remember, you may select as a focus of your presentation any artist who is covered in the text. The person you select should be one who particularly appeals to you. However, you should not pick an artist whom the syllabus indicates we will be covering in class. For example, you might choose Marcel DuChamps, Roualt, or Rousseau.

B. Covering Important Areas

As you consider your artist, you should be concerned with such areas as biography, technique, influences on the artist, and the artist's contribution to other artists and to the culture in general. For your report you can decide just which of these areas are of real interest and are of significance.

C. Doing Research

Once you have selected an artist, make an appointment to see me. Be prepared to explain why you chose whom you did. At that point I will direct you to sources that you can read in order to formulate a statement of purpose. For example, if you said you were interested in Pissarro I would tell you to review Impressionism by Phoebe Poole, History of Impressionism by John Rewald, and Pissarro, also by Rewald. In addition, I would ask you to look over the bibliographies in each of these books and to consult any other sources that you think might be interesting.

Figure 10.4   Developed from the work of Marguerita Grecco.

D. Taking Focused Notes and Recording Sources

Don't take notes on everything you read, only things about the artist and his works which support or question the point you said you want to make. For example, there's no sense in noting that Pissarro's father painted draperies unless you find that is how his son learned to paint. You need not copy information down word for word unless it's a quote you may want to incorporate into your presentation. Be sure also to take notes on any thoughts you yourself might have as you do your research. Finally, be sure to copy down bibliographic information in the appropriate form.

When we meet we'll also discuss the best way to organize your material and possible slides you might use.

E. Limiting the Topic and Developing a Statement of Purpose

Once you have the sources to review, you should preview them in an effort to come up with a statement about the author which you think is interesting. This statement, which should be no longer than one sentence, will form the basis of your presentation and will express the main point you want to make. For example, your purpose statement might read: "Although Pissarro is not the most well-known impressionist, because of his encouraging support of other artists of his time, he is often considered the father or master of the impressionists."

Write your purpose statement on a 5 x 8 index card and turn it in to me by March 15. I will review it and return it to you with comments.

F. Developing Cue Cards

By the week of April 20th you should review your notes and reorganize them where necessary on 5 x 8 cards, in cue card format. That is, write out your purpose statement so you can keep it well in mind. Below the statement, outline the information you want to present in the order you want to present it. Except for the purpose statement and any direct quotes, your notes should be a combination of phrases and clauses--not complete sentences. Mark with an asterisk any place you want to show a slide, note its title perhaps in different color ink, and arrange your slides for presentation.

Figure 10.4 (continued)

G.   "Proofing" Your Presentation

Practice your presentation by talking it through aloud
from your cue cards. It's not uncommon for students
to fear that on the day of their presentation, they'll
forget what to say. In an attempt to allay their
fears, often they try to write out their speech. Don't
do it! If your speech sounds canned, it will not be
accepted for a grade. Further, if you read from your
cards, you may put us all to sleep. Practice a
minimum, of five times. As you talk through your
presentation from your notes over and over again, you
probably will find that the pieces will begin to fall
together. There may be phrases that sound particularly
good and you will want to make note of them or underline them if they already appear on your cue cards.
(You may also find you need to reorganize some of the
notes on your cue cards.) After several run-throughs,
practice giving your speech again but this time
synchronized to your slides. Then, when you think you
are ready, make an audiotape and "proof" your speech;
using the Self-Assessment Form attached, take notes on
it in terms of content and form. Pretend you are the
instructor grading your presentation, complete the
form, and hand it in with your cue cards on the day of
your presentation.

Due: May 1

III.   Anticipating Responses to Your Presentation

There will be at least two different types of responses
to your presentation. (A) You should expect oral
comments and questions (from the class and from me)
to which you must respond. Again, it would be helpful
for you to use your Self-Assessment Form and actually
try to identify and practice answering such questions,
for in class I will grade you not only on the form and
content of your speech but also on your ability to
respond to questions. (B) Then I will share with
you the notes I took on your presentation and give you
a copy of my assessment form.

Figure 10.4 (continued)

11 | Providing Helpful Reactions to Students' Oral Responses in Class

Overview

Behind much of the classical concern for oratory was the notion that speech was a tool of public persuasion and public policy. Although few of us today would recommend oral training for students in such formal areas as style, elocution, and gesture, most of us would agree that how we talk (along with what we say) influences whether or not people understand us and often whether or not they take us seriously.

Developing lines of reasoning and delivering these effectively, however, are skills that need development over time. No one course or experience can provide sufficient training. Even the more traditional speech curriculum that requires students to prepare and to deliver a set number of speeches, though helping to develop important speaking skills, does not provide the steady, focused attention necessary. Such a speech course may lay the groundwork, but it is in the disciplines where attention to performance takes on real meaning as students offer thoughts and information, as they formulate opinions aloud and marshal arguments, as they ask significant questions. It is in this setting that students need ongoing feedback on their ability to organize ideas, on their development of these ideas, on the syntax and style of their discourse—in short, on the content- and form-related oral skills that make up classroom interaction. (See Strategy 2 for identification of some of these skills.) For such attention to what students say and how they say it will help prepare them for the kind of discussion in academic settings and in professional situations they will face in the future.

Now, while it is easy enough to monitor student performance in formal speaking situations, some teachers feel uneasy about approaching, in a public way, an area as sensitive as individual, informal speech. After all, everyone is listening. The real challenge, then, is to respond to ongoing discourse in a supportive way that advances communication, that furthers the flow of ideas and information. While our responses to students' comments can cover a wide range of areas from the deeper regions of content and logic to the more surface regions such as pronunciation and grammar, our style of responding must remain steadily constructive as we call attention both to the positive elements and to the problem areas. While initially this may be hard to do, with practice teachers can develop a repertoire of techniques to help students become aware of and address ongoing problems in their communication. It is important that students have a sense of how well their responses are

110

answering the question at hand, how deeply they are going, how well their presentation (their pronunciation, their grammar, their volume, etc.) is advancing their purpose. Drawing attention to problem areas will help make clear those patterns that may hold students back in their college work, and perhaps also in their careers, and will help ensure that skills in these areas are strengthened. Then, too, objectifying strengths in what students say and in how well they say it will reinforce these strengths and set them apart as models for other students.

Strategy 11: Providing Helpful Reactions to Students' Oral Responses in Class

Step 1: Review critical "form" and "content" oral skills. The give and take of classroom interaction is key to learning. Productive interaction, though, depends upon good speaking and good listening skills, and the development of such skills requires constant attention and reinforcement. But before discussing techniques for attending to students' oral skills, we need to look at the range of skills we may want to address. As you will recall from Strategy 2, students' oral communication skills can be thought of as either content-related skills or form-related skills. To review, content-related skills include such abilities as distinguishing fact from opinion, providing personal reactions when appropriate, drawing generalizations from information and examples, giving focused responses, and providing in-depth analyses when needed. Another way to look at these skills is to reflect upon what we hear when students do not exhibit them. They tend to offer opinions when the discussion requires facts and details, concentrate on the ideas and feelings of others when the request is for their own reactions, provide personalized examples when the discussion calls for broad conclusions, shift topics and not answer the question asked, and give surface answers and not take a topic far enough really to answer the question. Form-related oral skills include using silent pauses while thinking through ideas, making use of the voice (volume) to carry a point, pronouncing words correctly, using words correctly, using appropriate grammar, and organizing ideas logically. To look at these skills another way is to reflect upon what we hear when students do not exhibit them. They tend to make excessive use of verbal fillers such as "like" and "you know," speak too softly to be heard or to have credibility, eliminate/add syllables or distort certain sounds, use words inappropriately, use nonstandard English where standard grammar is expected, and organize ideas illogically.

Step 2: Identify the particular form and content features of students' oral interaction which you will want to reinforce or to which you will want students to pay particular attention. With these "form" and "content" skills clearly in mind, you will next want to identify both the particular skills you want to reinforce and the problem areas to which you want to draw your students' attention. To do this you can do two things. (a) Before the term begins, you can reflect on the kind of oral interaction generally occurring in your course and draw up a list of strengths and problem areas that stand out in your mind from students' past perform-ances. For example, you might recall that among students' strengths was a readiness to punctuate a point by sharing personal feelings. How-ever, you might also recall that some students tended to give opinions when facts were requested or tended to give surface answers when depth was required. Then, too, while many students seemed to organize ideas logically, they may have tended to make excessive use of verbal fillers. (b) Then, after class gets underway, you can refer to your notes, in which you recorded problem areas emerging during the first few weeks of class (see Strategy 2) and modify your list to reflect particular class and individual student needs. These two procedures should give you a fairly complete list of skills to focus on.

*Step 3: Review some of the techniques for reacting to students' oral responses.** There are many ways to draw students' attention to what they say and how they say it. Some methods are particularly good for attending to content skills, some to form skills, and some to both. Some are relatively easy to implement in any situation; others have certain requirements. Some of these methods can be used solely by you, while others may be used by students, too, or by some combination of them and you. The methods discussed below are but a few of those that teachers have found effective.

Let us assume that your students exhibit some of the content-related problems in oral skills discussed in Strategy 2, problems indicating that students have not provided the precise response demanded by questions. Two obvious techniques to draw students' attention to an inappropriate answer are:

- To repeat the question slowly and deliberately.
- To use a follow-up question that incorporates a cue word in order to focus attention on requested information.

Neither of these techniques breaks the flow of discussion, and both prob-ably are part of your usual method of response. The important thing to remember, though, is that students recognize that a question you repeat or follow up with a "directive" makes a comment about the initial response.

In addition to repeating questions and asking follow-up questions, there are other methods that call attention to the problem in a more direct way. One such technique is to "mirror" the part of a response that indicates that the speaker has not really supplied the requested infor-mation. Consider, for example, the following interaction in which an art

* Adapted from the work of Jim Weaver.

teacher is trying to help a student focus on description rather than on evaluation.

Teacher: How would you describe Picasso's "Guernica"?
Student: I hated it.
Teacher: Hated?
Student: The painting has . . .

Some teachers like this approach because it zeroes in on the problem but it does not supply the "right" answer, requiring instead that the student find his or her own way once the problem is identified. The "mirroring" technique is effective as well in helping students identify problems in "form" skills. In fact, repeating mispronunciations, nonstandard forms, or verbal fillers such as "you know" can become an activity carried on by students themselves, and with adequate introduction, the technique can be very revealing. For example, students hearing themselves and their peers (and their teacher, perhaps) repeating "you know" again and again come to see just how pervasive such oral patterns really are. This ear-training is important in helping students develop control over their spoken language. It should be noted, however, that this technique is most effective if the teacher and students agree on particular oral behaviors to mirror and agree on particular students to do the mirroring.

Another possible technique for monitoring oral behavior is to identify the type of response given and then to remind the speaker of the intent of original question:

Teacher: How would you describe . . . ?
Student: I hated it.
Teacher: I hear you have a strong reaction, but you're giving an opinion. Try to describe the formal features of the painting that made you react so strongly.
Student: The painting has . . .

This technique not only signals that there is a problem, as did the first three techniques, but also has the added advantage of explaining just what the problem is and, thus, may help students reach for appropriate solutions.

Another technique involves locating aloud the problem for students. For example, instead of mirroring or identifying a problem in form, some teachers will simply repeat the sentence up to the point where the problem occurred.

Student: He axed an impossible question.
Teacher: He . . .
Student: He asked . . .

"Locating," like mirroring and identifying, has the advantage of focusing student attention on the problem without correcting it for them.

The examples provided above in no way exhaust techniques for attending to students' speech. Some teachers will prefer to speak to the student after class about a detected problem in oral communication. Although this kind of private conference keeps the problem between teacher and student, the delay between the time of the error and the time it is identified may limit the effectiveness of this technique. Besides, the process of attending to oral skills need not be embarrassing if it is first introduced thoughtfully and if it becomes a regular class activity during which students monitor the teacher's oral skills too. Obviously, the technique you choose will in some ways relate both to the skills on which you will focus and to the assumptions you have about your students' oral skills. For example, if you are not sure whether your students are able to recognize a particular problem either in form or content, you probably will not want to use "mirroring," which merely calls a student's attention to the fact that there is a problem, but rather you may want to use the technique of "identifying" because it will help the particular student to understand just what the problem is.

Whatever technique or combination of techniques you use—whether you call attention to a problem by focusing on the original question or by focusing on the response—clue students in to the problem in a nonevaluative way. (See also the distinction between evaluative and descriptive comments when responding to students' papers, as discussed in Strategy 6.) This is important because it allows the student to concentrate on the behavior. On the other hand, evaluative statements about effective oral skills are a very productive way to call attention to such skills and to reinforce them. A well-turned phrase, a well-supported opinion deserves recognition. But here, too, it makes sense to support your reaction with a statement that helps students see what exactly seemed so positive. A comment such as "Good, you really supported your opinion with solid facts," will give the student much more than the mere pat on the back of a "good" alone and will allow the speaker and the other students to learn from the moment.

Step 4: Decide how and when you will tell the class of your intentions (and methods) for attending to oral skills. The activities described above are aural editing activities that require students to listen actively to what they and others say. Like editing in writing, these activities can be used to pinpoint a variety of oral behaviors, from lack of clarity to nonstandard forms. Like proofreading in writing, to be most productive, these monitoring techniques should probably not be performed by the teacher exclusively but rather should involve students' active participation. All these techniques require, then, a full understanding by your students of procedures and goals. To make students part of the process, you will need to decide when to introduce particular techniques and how to go about doing so. At the very minimum, you will want to develop a clear statement which indicates your expectations of students in class discussion and which describes how students will get feedback on their participation. Such a statement could be shared with students orally, during the first week of class, or included in a learning guide which you distribute. See the statements in the sample learning guide at the end of this text.

Part IV

Strategies for Helping Students Read Successfully in Content Courses

12 | Previewing Readings

Overview

The anxiety attendant to new and unknown situations is commonplace, as is the easing of this anxiety once the situation becomes known. The classroom is no exception, and for some students, facing a new textbook can be one of those anxiety-producing situations. Both the advances of knowledge and the sophisticated information systems we have for recording and reporting these advances have made the content matter of many texts more complicated than ever before. There is an enormous quantity of material writers must present to their student audiences. Indeed, even before students look at what lies within, a textbook can threaten them by its size alone and, unfortunately, can seem instead of a window to knowledge, a door shut against it.

Modern technology and strong editorial support from the best educational publishers, however, have improved methods of presenting material in textbooks. Design, layout, typography, illustrations—these contribute significantly to the content of a text by making ideas and data more accessible to readers. Most texbooks, then, are written and presented in a very organized manner with special features—some overt, some more subtle—to assist readers in dealing with the information at hand. Alerting students to these features can help students to feel more in control of what might have seemed an overwhelming task—mastering the text. For many students on their own do not know how to make the technical features of a book serve them.

The steps in the following strategy will guide you in creating an activity to help your students preview the text or other assigned readings for your course. By previewing—becoming familiar with the special divisions, features, and layout of a written work—students can better deal with the complex material your course may demand. Previewing is, of course, no replacement for thoughtful reading. It is, however, a way of helping to establish conditions that encourage it.

Strategy 12: Previewing Readings

Step 1: Review the process of previewing. Previewing is looking at and thinking about the important parts of reading material before starting to read. Let us consider for a minute what most of us do when we look at a text for the first time, perhaps one we are considering for adoption in a course we will be teaching. Odds are most of us look first at the table of contents (although the cover of the book has obviously already suggested some message about its content). We will use the table of contents to help us predict the topics covered by the book. Section and chapter titles, subtitles, headings, and subheadings will let us know how the book relates to the units of material we want to cover. Perhaps we will check in the index for a major concept that does not leap out at us. Then we may notice a photograph, illustration, or table. We may look at the preface to see the writer's goals and orientation and to determine just how closely they concur with our own.

Most practiced readers survey new books in a similar way. Unfortunately, many students have not learned how this act of previewing can help them learn about the content of a text. Certainly, knowing about the title, the author's preface or foreword, the table of contents, the index, the appendix, the glossary, and the bibliography will help students use their texts more efficiently than they have in the past, as will learning how to examine each assigned chapter for its special features (title, introduction, headings, subheadings, running heads, special typographical effects, summary statements, questions). Yet more importantly, previewing will help students begin to learn the subject matter of the course.

Suppose, for example, that your course is Introduction to Chemistry and that by the second or third class you want to get to systems of measurement and then to the relationship between mass and weight, among other things. Certainly, you could lecture on the English and the metric systems and on the role of gravity in the computation of weight. But you also could help students use the technique of previewing to begin to learn those concepts or others like them. In *Basic Concepts of Chemistry* by Sherman, Sherman, and Russikoff (Boston: Houghton Mifflin, 1980), Chapter 2 is called "Systems of Measurement, or Sizing Things Up"; the subheading, Section 2.4, appears in the index as "Mass and Weight." A clear graphic design—words in green boldface print with ruled green lines between them—provides definitions for mass and weight and offers a key for presentations of all definitions throughout the book. A formula appears, as do examples and solutions later on in the chapter. Furthermore, from point 6 on the list of learning goals at the start of Chapter 2, students know that after having read the chapter, they should be able to "distinguish between the mass of an object and the weight of an object." Self-test exercises at the chapter's end offer practice in calculations related to the new concept; answers appear in a back section of the book. The index identifies page numbers for "mass," and a concise definition of the term appears again in a glossary in Supplement D. Thus a student who uses previewing techniques will soon realize that it is both the special features of the whole book and the special features of individual chapters which offer important clues to information in the text.

An instructor showing the class how to preview *Basic Concepts of Chemistry* would make that aim incidental to instruction in a key concept required for understanding the course. Learning about mass, weight, and gravity, students at the same time can learn how their textbook delivers information, and they can be led to generalize about how this delivery system can help them learn other parts of the course. One of the really important benefits of previewing, then, is that it allows readers to acquire knowledge even before they read chapters in depth. Students can be trained to survey reading selections *before* reading them, and these surveys can increase the ultimate comprehension of course material.

Step 2: Review the various features of your text and a typical chapter, and make a list of those features that will help students use the book. While most texts include basic technical features (table of contents, index, glossary, and so on), others include many more features. Some of these will be more important for you than others. Beginning with the cover, identify and list *those technical features of your text that will be of most help to students in your course.* Do not assume that students know how to use any of these features, a glossary for example, or even know that these features exist. As you make your list, indicate the page on which each feature is found and, where appropriate, indicate any concepts or information that can be introduced at the same time that your students preview. For example, in a literature text, there may be a section on imagery (this can be gleaned from the table of contents), and you may wish to introduce the use of the glossary as well as the definition of

Technical Features	Page #	Related Concept or Information

Figure 12.1

imagery in your previewing activity. When you have determined the important features of your entire text, you then will want to review the features of a typical chapter and make a list of those features which seem most important. The chart in Figure 12.1 may be useful in completing this activity.

Step 3: Create an activity that guides students in using the important technical features both of your text as a whole and of an individual chapter of your text. With the important features of both in mind, plan two activities (one for the whole text and one for a chapter) to help students practice previewing while they learn about one or more concepts central to your course. The activity may be part of a class discussion or part of a home assignment. It can be written or oral. One thing to consider is the amount of class time the various formats could take. If your activity is to be written, you may want to include it as a homework assignment in the learning guide you prepare for students (see Strategy 15) so that you do not use important class time.

The activities you develop for previewing the text and individual chapters should be brief and may be introduced at the same time. Although the textbook as a whole will be previewed only once, you should consider previewing all reading matter you use. Your decision will depend on need, on the time available, on the length of the particular activities you select, and on your reaching the point at which you believe students can and should preview on their own. In Figure 12.2 are two sample activities,* one developed to preview an entire art text and the other developed to preview a typical chapter.

Although some students may not be able to distinguish accurately between chapters and units or other designators, previewing activities should lead to an understanding of these differences. Students should also have a better grasp of bold or italic print, footnotes, or information in parentheses.

When previewing is done as an in-class activity, teachers sometimes find that some students are already very proficient in using this skill. Two suggestions may help to avoid boredom on the part of these students: (a) create groups where the more proficient students can help others or (b) create questions dealing directly with concepts (but related to technical features), and have the more proficient students work on these.

Step 4: As a final step, it will be useful to review methods for previewing material without headings and subheadings. First, read and think about the title, the first and second paragraphs as well as the final paragraph or two, and the first sentences of all other paragraphs. Of course, if some textual features, such as pictures and charts, will help comprehension, these, too, should be considered. The idea here is that authors often present their main points in introductory material and in the first sentences of the body paragraphs and that they often summarize these points at

* Adapted from the work of Peter Brown.

<u>Getting to Know Your Text</u>

Text: <u>We Create ART Creates Us</u> by Duane Prebble

By becoming familiar with the textbook you will be using this quarter, you will be better able to use it. Preview the text as you answer the following questions.

1. Write the title of the text, and in two or three sentences explain what you think the title means.

   _____

   _____

   _____

   _____

   _____

2. Answer the following questions by finding and using the table of contents.

   a. On which pages is the table of contents? _____

   b. How many chapters are there in the text? _____

   c. What is the title of Chapter Three? _____

      _____

   d. What important art concept is discussed in Chapter Four and listed in Unit Two of the course syllabus?

      _____

      _____

      _____

3. Using the index, state on what pages you find a discussion of prehistoric art.

   _____

   _____

Figure 12.2

4. Using the table of contents, find where the bibliography begins. Then using the bibliography, locate other books that you could read to get more information on prehistoric art. Write three of the titles below.

_____

_____

_____

5. Look at page 187 and answer the following questions.

a. What is this section called? _____

b. Where is the painting "The Young Ladies Of Avignon" located?

_____

Previewing Chapter 1:

Answering the following questions will help familiarize you with the layout of the chapters in the text. Answer the questions in the blank spaces provided.

1. What is the title of Chapter One? _____

_____

2. Read the boldface headings found in Chapter One and briefly explain how they are connected with the title of the chapter.

_____

_____

3. Now list any similarities you see between the contents of this chapter and the film we saw, Why Man Creates.

_____

_____

4. Look at the illustration on page 5 and read paragraphs three and four on that page. Below, briefly explain how the text illustrations help us to understand its context.

_____

_____

Figure 12.2 (continued)

5. Skim page 16 in your text looking for the word "tone."
   Now look around the word to see if you can find its
   meaning in the context. Write the meaning of <u>tone</u> as
   it appears in the context.

   _____

   _____

6. Read the summary on page 29 and then list below the five
   criteria mentioned in Chapter One for determining "what
   art is."

   _____

   _____

   _____

   _____

   _____

Figure 12.2 (continued)

the end of a unit. By such selective reading, students should be able to
pick up and consider some of the main concepts before actually reading
in depth.

Previewing is an important learning strategy because it initiates
thinking and enables students to read with a purpose. Students should
preview their entire text, as a whole, and individual chapters as they
read. Previewing can also be applied to professional articles and newspapers. Students who preview will become more efficient readers,
increasing their concentration, comprehension, and memory. They will
know where their reading is taking them. They will be providing themselves with the conceptual framework needed to organize and absorb
new knowledge.

13 | Preparing Reading Guides

Overview

Have you ever started to read something and after several pages had to stop because you did not know what you had read? There are many reasons why this occurs. You may, perhaps, have had something on your mind that caused your attention to wander, or it may have been that the material was so new to you that as you concentrated on the pieces, you lost sight of the whole.

Students, too, when asked to identify their most pressing problems as readers, often say that they have difficulty concentrating. Their minds wander, and after reading a page or two, they say that they get lost in the details or that they cannot remember what they have read.

Previewing and building vocabulary (see Strategies 12 and 14 respectively) will certainly help students read with greater ease and comprehension. But these strategies may not be enough. Students may need guidance in focusing both on the main points of written material and on the ways in which these points relate to each other. One way to help students concentrate while they read is to provide them with a means of mentally organizing material as they read. One way to do this is to present "guide questions" for each of your major reading assignments. Guide questions are specially constructed questions that are given to students *before* they read to draw attention to important concepts or information in the assigned reading. When students review these guide questions in advance of reading, they establish a purpose for reading and should then be better able to focus on and to internalize what they read. The steps in the following strategy will help you develop guide questions for the assigned readings in your course.

Strategy 13: Preparing Reading Guides

Step 1: Review the language of reading guide "questions." You will want to give thought both to the scope and to the phrasing of reading guide questions. First, it is important to note that effective reading guide questions need not, grammatically speaking, be "questions." We are using the term *questions* loosely here to refer to any sentence that calls upon students to perform a particular mental operation as they read. Note, for example, that the question, "How will recent budget cuts affect higher education?" can also be stated as a directive, "List the effects of the budget cuts on higher education," or "Explain the effects of the budget cuts on higher education." Each of these "questions" can encourage students to perform and record important kinds of thinking.

The nature and the distinctions between "questions" and "directives" are examined at length in the discussion of Strategy 9. Here, however, it might be helpful to review a few of the more important points: the precision and the ambiguity inherent in the various "question words" and the use of "cue words" to focus questions and reading.

The question words *who, which, when*, and *where* are fairly explicit in the demands they make on potential respondents, whereas the words *how, why*, and sometimes *what* are not quite so clear-cut. For example, when we ask a question using the word *how*, we are asking students to perform several mental operations, some quite sophisticated. To answer the question, "How will recent budget cuts affect higher education?" students must call to mind the cuts, recognize cause-and-effect relationships, and then describe or explain these effects. Indeed, there may be times when such "open questions" are all the focus we want to give a particular reading. However, there may also be times when more focus would be helpful. This is when we would use "cue words" to develop directives which can be used in place of such questions or as "follow-up" to clarify the thinking certain questions are likely to elicit. It is important to remember, though, that when we limit our request by using certain "cue words" (for example, *list, identify*), we help to focus students' reading and responses, but we also limit those responses. The student asked to "list the effects of budget cuts on higher education" must call to mind cuts and determine those that are critical to higher education, but he or she will not have to explain or describe the effects. Both actual questions and directives can be helpful in their own way to guide students' reading, and you will need to decide which format best suits your purpose in a given situation.

Step 2: Identify and list the most important *ideas, concepts, and pieces of information that you wish students to know and understand from a particular reading assigned in a target unit of your course.* This may be done by simply underlining in your text or by preparing a list. The number of points you select obviously will be determined by what you want students to remember. If you are primarily interested in key concepts, your list may be quite short. If you want students to hold on to many details, your list will be longer.

Step 3: Write reading guide questions, and decide how to use them in your class. Using appropriate cue words and question words, develop "guide questions" to focus students' attention on the concepts, ideas, or pieces of information you have identified. Since it is helpful for students to see the relationships among ideas, concepts, and information, you also may want to consider grouping your reading guide items into categories reflecting these relationships.

Once you have developed this set of questions, or perhaps as you are developing these questions, you will want to decide how they best can be used in your course. First, you will want to decide when to distribute questions: whether to distribute this set of questions before the particular reading assignment; whether to include these questions with other sets of questions in a learning guide that you prepare for students and distribute at the start of the course; or whether to hand out this and other sets of questions for each new unit. Note, too, that guide questions can be used in class for many purposes beyond focusing students' attention as they read. They can be used to review material, to initiate class discussion, to provide a format for taking notes on readings, or to guide students in studying for exams. Two sample sets of guide questions (directives) are given below. One is taken from a learning guide for a course in accounting, and one is from a learning guide for a course in Latin American culture. Note that each set of questions is introduced by an explanation of how students are to use these questions.

A set of reading guide questions has been developed for each assignment in the course. These questions help you focus on the main points in each assignment. In your notebook, you should respond to these questions in your own words based on the information in your text. I will collect your responses to the reading guide questions from time to time and return them to you with appropriate comments.*

1. List two ways credit is used in the operations of many business enterprises.

2. Define the term *receivables*.

3. Define the term *payables*.

4. Compare the classification of receivables and payables in the balance sheet.

5. Define the term *contingent liabilities*.

6. Explain how a promissory note is used as a means of extending credit.

7. State the basic formula for computing simple interest.

8. Name the two kinds of notes that may be involved in discount transactions with a bank.

9. Describe the two generally accepted methods of accounting for receivables that are deemed to be uncollectible.

* From the work of Frank Timoni.

As you read tonight, think about each of the following questions. Then, when you have finished reading, answer each of the questions in the space provided on the back of this guide. No more than a paragraph or two is expected to provide a sufficient answer for any of the questions.*

1. Summarize the main issues in the Civil war between *unitarios* and *federales* in Argentina.

2. Who was Facundo Quiroga?

3. Restate Sarmiento's theory of "civilización y barbarie" as presented in *Facundo*.

4. Explain how Martí refutes Sarmiento's theories in "Nuestra América."

5. List the main provisions in Benito Juárez's Reform Laws (1857, 1862).

6. Evaluate the reign of Emperor Maximilian in Mexico in terms of his expectations and actual accomplishments.

In summary, then, a crucial need, seen both by students and teachers, is a method to help students to focus their reading. This need can be met by helping students prepare to read by reinforcing the skill of previewing and by preteaching vocabulary and concepts. Another way to meet this need is to present students with guide questions for key reading assignments. In this way, students will have help in focusing their attention while they are reading and develop, at the same time, the ability to offer responses that are clear and appropriate both in writing and in class discussion.

* From the work of Ana Maria Hernandez.

14 | Introducing Difficult Vocabulary

Overview

In recent years there has been a movement in the United States to simplify the language of contracts and other legal documents. Many people found themselves in a position of being unable to read materials that significantly affected their own lives. Lawyers—like government bureaucrats, scientists, and accountants—had developed their own language, which was incomprehensible to "outsiders."

While the extremes of technical and professional language are unnecessary, often serving the narrow interests of but a few, to some extent, in any field, technical language and technical use of existing language is bound to occur and is, in fact, important to the communication of ideas in that field. This is as true in education as it is in any other area. To gain access to the disciplines, we must master the vocabulary of those disciplines. As teachers, then, we may need to help students build a vocabulary that will enable them to understand and function in a subject area.

There are, however, misconceptions about the teaching and learning of vocabulary. Students do not really know new words (or concepts) until they can define and use them appropriately. Merely referring students to a glossary does not guarantee that they will learn pronunciation, meaning, or usage. For often the glossary is as difficult for them as the text itself. Then, too, having students rely exclusively on context clues or giving students new vocabulary after they have done the reading is not sufficient. For without being alerted to key vocabulary *before* they read, students can be frustrated in their reading as they stumble upon these new words or else simply overlook them and their importance to the assignment.

One way to introduce students to vocabulary is to include definitional questions as part of the set of guide questions you create for each reading assignment (see Strategy 13). There are, however, other ways, and the strategy below lays out steps to guide you in creating activities which will help students master new vocabulary and reinforce their new learning.

Strategy 14: Introducing Difficult Vocabulary

Step 1: Review the types of vocabulary that appear in textbooks. Vocabulary found in most course assignments can be classified as content or general vocabulary. *Content vocabulary* refers to those words that express concepts taught in the course. "Kinship" is an example of a "content word" that might appear in an anthropology text; a poetry text might present the word "meter"; a physics text might speak of "electrical energy." *General vocabulary*, on the other hand, consists of words that are not specifically related to any course content but make up part of our larger vocabulary and can present difficulties for students as well. As educators, then, we may find ourselves needing to help students learn both content and general vocabulary; and we may find ourselves needing to assist students as they develop their own vocabularies independently.

Step 2: Identify all the vocabulary words in a target unit that are important for students to know. That is, decide which words are important but may be new and prove difficult for students. These words can come primarily from readings but also can be vocabulary used in lectures or class discussions. As mentioned earlier, some of these words will be important because they represent concepts that you wish students to learn. Identify and then make a list of these new words.

Step 3: Decide which of the identified words are essential *and need to be introduced to students* before *they read the text.* As you go through the reading for a target unit, you will probably come up with a rather extensive list of vocabulary words which will be new to students. Giving students such a list, however, can be overwhelming and may prove counterproductive. Therefore, you may need to narrow your original list down to the words that are essential for students to know and understand before they read, so that they can read with comprehension. The remaining words on your extensive list can be handled in other ways, for example, by reviewing with students the use of context clues, the glossary in a text, or the dictionary.

Step 4: Develop an activity for introducing key vocabulary to students. There are many ways to introduce vocabulary to students before they begin the reading assignment. One way is simply to distribute or write on the board your list of key words, reviewing pronunciation, meaning, and usage. Or you can require that students, once given a vocabulary list for a particular reading, work through the list on their own. Still another approach is to construct a diagram that presents the interrelationship of key vocabulary terms. Notice how the word list in Figure 14.1 is transformed into a structural overview of a potential lesson. An assignment, then, might be for students to define the relationship which the various terms have to each other and then to discuss these relationships briefly in class.

Step 5: Develop activities to help students learn new vocabulary on their own. Students will not always be able to depend on a teacher to help

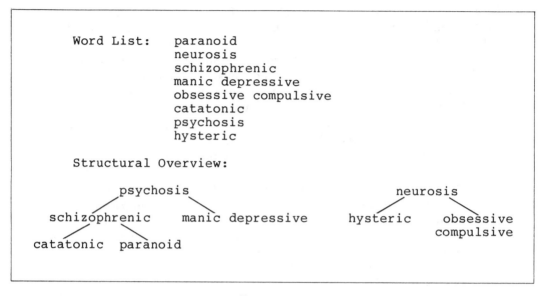

Figure 14.1

them learn new vocabulary. They need to develop independence in learning new words, and you can help them develop this independence by giving them practice in certain vocabulary development skills.

Often, students will visually recognize a word only after they hear it pronounced. Therefore, students should be encouraged to try to pronounce new words they come across. There is a chance they will recognize these words if they come fairly close to their correct pronunciation. For example, if a student has heard the word *mortgage* but has never read it, pronouncing it might bring him or her close enough to recognize it.

Students also should be made aware that most textbooks set off important vocabulary and key concepts in dark print or in italics with the definition usually nearby. In addition, students can be encouraged to use context clues to develop new vocabulary. There are four major types of context clues that authors employ.* Readers who are trained to recognize them will comprehend more fully, develop their vocabulary more naturally, and save time because they will not have to look new words up in a dictionary.

Clue 1. Synonym. The same idea is expressed by two or three different words or phrases.

Example: After a meeting like that, Eric was certain he would have to endure many *inane* and pointless discussions.

---

* Adapted from *Learning to Learn* by Donald E. P. Smith et al. (New York: Harcourt, Brace & World, 1961), pp. 125–131.

Clue 2. Definition. A word is described or defined by the words around it.

Example: The old factory was now *defunct*. It had seen its best days and was no longer in operation.

Clue 3. Comparison and Contrast. The context may tell the meaning of a word by telling what it does not mean or by comparing it with a familiar word.

Example: Roosevelt was noted for his *succinct* and effective speech. Truman, conversely, used many words to express his ideas.

Clue 4. Summary. After a situation or idea is presented, the author sums it up with one word. We can learn the new word by understanding what it is summarizing.

Example: Beth could not decide whether to pursue a new career. Her *quandary* made her depressed and difficult to live with.

Finally, keep the text glossary or the dictionary in mind. If students fail to find the meaning of a word by pronouncing it or using the context, then they can be encouraged to use an appropriate reference guide.

In summary, then, students may need our help in order to master the language and vocabulary of our subjects. When we offer assistance in vocabulary before the class reads difficult material, we improve students' chances for reading with comprehension and for learning and thinking about course content. Further, by encouraging students to develop and practice vocabulary skills on their own, we are helping them with skills that they can use in other courses and in many other areas of their lives as well.

Part V

Integrating Language Skills for Content Mastery

15 | A Holistic Approach to Content: Integrated Skills Reinforcement (ISR)

Overview

The "guide" for this text suggests several ways that the materials in this book can be used. They can be used to address a particular problem area, reading, perhaps, or listening or writing or oral communication. Here you choose the appropriate assessment strategy and then select other strategies to help students deal more effectively with course content despite the difficulties they may experience when functioning in that linguistic mode. Another way, however, is what we have called "integrated skills reinforcement," the ISR approach. This approach involves building all the strategies for reinforcing reading, writing, oral, and listening skills into your course. If you selected the latter approach, you will recall that it was suggested that you begin by creating materials that apply all the strategies to a target unit. Let us assume here that you have already done this. Let us assume, too, that you have been able to experience on a small scale the interrelationships among the skills and the ways in which they can be used to aid student learning. You may have seen, for example, how a reading assignment involving guide questions can become a writing assignment as students answer these questions on paper and, in turn, how these reading and writing assignments can become the basis for oral activities such as class discussion and presentations. These oral activities can, in turn, become points of departure for further reading, writing, or speaking. Thus the integrated approach helps students come to the content of a course from many angles. And operating together, the various angles, the various linguistic modes, encourage thinking in and about a discipline in a systematic and critical way.

The strategy presented below will take you beyond your early "target" unit to consider your course as a whole. First, we suggest ways to expand your activities so that other units in your course offer opportunities for reading, writing, speaking, and listening as a means for knowing and understanding subject matter. Next, we suggest methods for clarifying for students the general requirements for using each of the skills areas—what students are to do when faced with *any* reading, writing, or oral communication assignment in your course. Finally, the strategy describes how to gather together the materials (course description, objectives, syllabus, and so on) you generally distribute in your course, as well as materials you developed as a result of work with this book, into a learning guide. This is a document of materials that will guide students to use all their language skills to explore and master course content.

Many teachers and students like having such a learning guide at the start of the course because it provides clear direction for the course, both for specific assignments and for general course requirements. Some teachers, however, prefer to distribute the particular assignment sheets as the need for them arises during the course. Whichever approach you decide on—a single document or a collection of materials from which to draw—you will do well to have the materials prepared before the course begins. Such materials serve the purpose of letting students know where they must go and how they are to get there. The following steps will help you develop a learning guide for your course.

Strategy 15: A Holistic Approach to Content: Integrated Skills Reinforcement (ISR)

Step 1: Review the range of activities (suggested in previous strategies) for helping students make more effective use of the expressive (speaking, writing) and the receptive (listening, reading) modes of language in learning course content. Reviewing is necessary before you can decide where it might be useful to build additional activities into your course beyond your "target" unit—the unit you selected as a focus for your early work. For reference, the kinds of assignments you will be considering include:

1. For reading—previewing of chapters and articles, guide questions, vocabulary exercises (Strategies 12, 13, 14).
2. For writing—brief writing assignments, formal papers, field and lab reports (Strategies 5, 7, 8).
3. For oral/aural communication—questions to promote active listening during lectures and questions to guide purposeful discussion, brief and/or formal oral assignments, activities for attending to students' oral responses in class (Strategies 9, 10, 11).

Step 2: Review your present course syllabus, and decide where additional reading, writing, and oral/aural communication activities would facilitate further learning. Begin by noting on your syllabus, for your own reference, the places where you have developed assignments for the target unit. Then decide where you think it would be helpful to develop additional reading, writing, and oral/aural communication activities to help students master course content. A sample annotated syllabus is presented in Figure 15.1. Notice how the instructor indicates particular activities designed to enhance communications strategies.

INTRODUCTION TO ART

Jan. 2   Introduction to Course *skills assessment activities*
           Film: Why Man Creates *preview of text*
                                    brief written summary of

Jan. 4   Art Project *introduction of activities*   *film*
                    for attending to students' oral responses in class

Jan. 9   Lecture/Discussion (Ch. 1) *preview of chapter and*
                      preview plan for rest of chapter

Jan. 11   Discussion (Ch. 2, pp. 30–34) *guide questions and*
                    vocabulary activities for rest of readings

Jan. 16   Lecture/Discussion (Ch. 2, pp. 35–65) *focus and*
                   discussion questions for rest of class

Jan. 18   Discussion (Ch. 2, pp. 66–72)

Jan. 23   Lecture/Discussion (Ch. 3, pp. 73–98) *additional*
                   written museum report

Jan. 25   Discussion (Ch. 3, pp. 99–113)

Jan. 30   Lecture/Discussion (Ch. 3, pp. 114–132) *brief*
                   oral presentation on painting

Feb. 1   Quiz (Ch. 1–3) *3 short essay questions for quiz*

Feb. 6   Lecture/Discussion (Ch. 4, pp. 157–165)

Feb. 13   No Class

Feb. 15   Discussion (Ch. 4, pp. 166–177) *museum report*
              Assign Museum Visit

Feb. 20   Lecture/Discussion (Ch. 5, pp. 178–200)

Feb. 27   Lecture/Discussion (Ch. 5, pp. 200–211) *brief*
                   oral presentation for art project

Mar. 1   No Class

Mar. 6   Lecture/Discussion (Ch. 5, pp. 212–232)

Mar. 8   Museum Report Due
              Discussion of Reports

Mar. 13   Discussion (Ch. 6, pp. 233–242)
              Art Project
              Final Portfolio Due

Mar. 15   Final Exam *essay question for final exam*

Figure 15.1

Step 3: List the specific reading, writing, and aural/ oral communication activities you will include in your course. Working from the syllabus you have marked, develop a list of the activities you identified. Your list will include, of course, both activities and assignments you have already developed from working in this book as well as those that you will need to develop for the remainder of the course.

Consider the following sample lists developed from the preceding syllabus.

Reading Activities

1. Assessment activities
2. Previewing activity for entire text (written)
3. Previewing activity for Chapter 1 (written)
4. Fourteen sets of guide statements for fourteen reading assignments
5. Previewing activity for five remaining chapters (oral)
6. Vocabulary activities for fourteen reading assignments

Writing Activities

1. Assessment activity—paragraph on expectations (first day)
2. Museum Report #1
3. Three short essays included in quiz on Chapters 1–3
4. Museum Report #2
5. Three-page essay included in final exam

Oral/Aural Communications Activities

1. Assessment activities
2. Introduction of activities used to attend to students' oral responses in class
3. Focus questions for fifteen lectures
4. Discussion questions for fifteen class meetings
5. Brief oral presentation

Step 4: Develop needed assignments and materials, and revise your syllabus. Now, based on your list of projected activities, develop the assignments and materials needed beyond your "target" unit. Write the remainder of reading guide questions for your text, for example; add your additional brief writing assignments, perhaps or some guidelines for a research paper; develop focus questions for class lectures; and so on. Then revise your syllabus to reflect this work.

Step 5: Create general statements summarizing the nature and scope of reading, writing, and oral communication assignments in your course. In addition to clearly stated directions for each of the assignments you created, students also need an overview of the nature and number of assignments, along with a sense of how to proceed in general when faced with a reading, a writing, or an oral communication assignment in the course.

For the reading component in your instruction, develop a general statement about the reading assignments—how many, what texts, and so on—followed by an explanation of any activities that accompany reading assignments—these include previewing, answering reading guide questions, and completing vocabulary exercises. (For examples of general statements on reading, see the general reading requirements section included in the sample learning guide at the end of this text.)

You will want to create a similar statement to explain the writing requirements for your course. This statement should tell students how many writing assignments they must complete, the steps to follow in preparing a manuscript, the attention students must pay to editing and proofreading, and so forth. (For examples of general statements on writing see the general writing requirements sections included in the sample learning guide.)

Finally, you should prepare a general statement on the aural/oral requirements for the course. This statement should make clear the nature and number of assignments, the students' responsibilities in class discussion, techniques for attending to students' oral responses in class, and the general steps to follow for any oral presentations. (See the sample learning guide.)

Step 6: Develop a means of gathering general and skills-related information from students. In the first section of this text, you examined strategies for gauging the level of students'skills in relation to your course requirements. As you may recall, one way to get a sense of students' skills levels is to determine which, if any, skills courses students were required to take in advance of your course. To gather this information quickly with reference to all the skills areas, you may want to develop a questionnaire for distribution to students during the first week of class. Such a questionnaire may merely be an adaptation of that format you already use for gathering general information about students (names, addresses, phone numbers, majors, and so on.) You may want to look at the questionnaire included in the sample learning guide that follows this strategy. The student questionnaire is a good place in which to include space for a brief writing sample, one of the important instruments for assessment.

Step 7: Identify the materials you want students to have both at the start of the course and as the course proceeds. You will want to share with your students many of the materials you have created thus far. Look over your materials, and decide which ones students need. Some materials (the Fry readability graph, ongoing class discussion questions, essays for exams, etc.) are for your purposes only and would not be distributed to the class.

For review, student-oriented materials may include:

- Skills assessment materials (where appropriate)
- General statements on reading, writing, and oral/aural activities in the course
- Guide statements for reading assignments
- Vocabulary activities
- Previewing activities (if written)
- Assignment sheets for *each* writing assignment
- Assignment sheets for any formal oral presentations (and for oral brief activities, where appropriate)
- Focus questions to foster active listening
- Forms you developed to give students feedback on writing and/or oral assignments
- Self-assessment forms for such assignments

Whether or not you will be distributing these materials in a packet or as students need them, you will want them all ready for use before the course begins.

Step 8: Gather together other materials you generally distribute in your course. Along with the materials just developed, you will want to gather together those materials that you routinely distribute at the start of a course—syllabus, course objectives, grading information, and so on. Based upon your work from the principles in this book, you may have to revise some of these materials.

Step 9: Decide on a schedule and a method for distributing the various materials to students. As we noted before, many people find it useful to distribute course materials in a booklet or in a packet at the start of the course—even materials the student will not need until late in the term. Some teachers, however, prefer to distribute an introductory packet early in the term and to make the rest of the materials available for distribution as needed. The important thing is to have materials, and clear explanations of them, prepared in advance of the course and to plan when you will be using them in class. Decide, then, what you will be distributing at what point in the course.

Step 10: Create a learning guide consisting of those materials you will need at the start of the course and as the course proceeds. Whatever your distribution schedule may be, now gather together all the materials we have discussed. The learning guide that follows for a course in statistics shows how these materials come together; the guide was designed for distribution at the start of the term. The following sample table of contents in Figure 15.2, annotated to suggest possible materials to include, may be helpful as you think about ways of organizing your own materials.

Figure 15.2

       writing and your expectation that they move through
these stages as they develop assignments; tell them
about proofreading, present an error inventory or
proofreading sheet with an explanation of how you
and they will use it. Explain the use of due dates,
etc.)

Oral/Aural . . . .
(You might include here first the statement you
created on the nature of oral communication in your
course and on the number and nature of specific
assignments. You might also explain relevant procedures, e.g., what class participation means in
the course, how discussion will proceed, the interrelationship, if any, of reading guide questions to
class discussion, etc.)

IV.   GRADING . . . .

V.   ASSIGNMENTS AND MATERIALS
(You may want to present both vocabulary and reading
guides as well as writing and oral assignments in an
"integrated" way, unit by unit.)

Previewing Activities (if written) . . . .
    For text . . . .
    For chapter . . . .
Reading Guide Questions . . . .
Vocabulary Activities . . . .
(These may be integrated with Reading Guide ques-
tions.)
Writing Activities . . . .
(Include here actual assignment sheets you developed,
student samples, examples of your own writing, etc.)
Oral/Aural Activities . . . .
(Include actual assignment sheets and self-assessment
forms, sets of focus questions for each class session,
etc.)

Figure 15.2 (continued)

A Learning Guide for Elementary Statistics

(with supplemental materials for instructor's use—
not to be given to students)

*Prepared by Anthony P. Giangrasso, Ph.D., Mathematics Department,
LaGuardia Community College, City University of New York.*

Contents

I. GENERAL COURSE INFORMATION

A. Text. Understanding Statistics: Concepts and Methods by Brase and Brase, Heath Publishing Company, 1978.

B. Catalogue Description. 3 Periods, 3 Credits
A study of the basic concepts and computational techniques of elementary statistics. Among the topics studied are: measures of central tendency, standard deviation, percentiles, statistical graphs, normal distribution, probability, and hypothesis testing.

C. ISR Method. In this course, besides learning statistics, students will be encouraged to reinforce their reading, writing, oral, aural, and basic mathematics skills as well. This approach to teaching is called Integrated Skills Reinforcement (ISR).

D. Entry-Level Skills. The student should have computational ability with whole numbers, fractions, decimals, percents, and signed numbers. Students should be familiar with formula substitution.

E. Pre- and Corequisites. MAT099 is a prerequisite, and CSE098 is a corequisite for elementary statistics. This ensures that the student has been at least introduced to algebra and that he or she can read at least on the 9th grade level.

F. Instructional Objectives. To examine the principles of collecting data, study the graphical organization and numerical summarization of data, examine the basic rules of probability, study probability distributions of random variables, study the normal distribution and its use as an approximation to the binomial distribution, be introduced to hypothesis testing.

G. Performance Objectives. The students will learn to:

1. Calculate the mean, mode, median, and range.
2. Calculate standard deviation from raw and grouped data.
3. Construct frequency distributions and histograms.
4. Calculate simple probabilities.
5. Calculate binomial and normal probabilities.
6. Approximate the binomial with the normal distribution.
7. Apply the concept of the central limit theorem.
8. Calculate and intrepret the correlation coefficient.
9. Test for independence using chi square.
10. Test hypotheses involving the mean.

H. Syllabus.

Date	Meeting Number	Reading Assignment Section	Topic
Mar. 29	1	1	Introduction
30	2	2.1	Random Samples
Apr. 1	3	2.2	Graphs
5	4	2.3	Frequency Distributions and Histograms
6	5	3.1	Averages
12	6	3.2	Variations
13	7	3.3	Standard Deviation
15	8	3.3	Standard Deviation
19	9	4.1	Probability
20	10	4.2	Probability Rules
22	11	4.3	Probability Distributions
26	12	4.3	Probability Distributions
27	13	9.1	Scatter Diagrams
29	14	9.3	Correlation Coefficient
May 3	15	9.3	Correlation Coefficient
4	16	5.1	Binomial Experiments
6	17	5.2	Binomial Distributions
10	18	5.3	Binomial Distributions
11	19	5.3	Binomial Distributions
13	20	10.1	Chi Square
17	21	6.1	Normal Distribution
18	22	6.2	Standard Units
20	23	6.3	Areas under the Normal Curve
24	24	6.4	Central Limit Theorem
25	25	6.5	Normal Approximation to the Binomial
27	26	8.1	Hypothesis Testing
June 3	27	8.2	Tests Involving the Mean
7	28	8.2	Tests Involving the Mean
8	29	–	Final Exam
10	30	–	Summary and Evaluation

I. Due Dates for the Steps of the Research Paper.

Date	Meeting Number	Due
Apr. 5	4	Method of Data Collection
Apr. 20	10	Organization of the Data
Apr. 29	14	Statistical Description of the Data
May 10	18	Obtaining the Correlation Coefficient
May 18	22	Testing for Independence with Chi Square
June 10	30	Testing the Mean Summary of the Results

II. STUDENT INFORMATION

A. Student Questionnaire

Name _____ Soc. Sec. # _____

Address _____

Phone (Home) _____ (Work) _____

Counselor's Name _____

Major _____

Do you plan to continue your education at a 4-year college?

[ ] yes   [ ] no

. . . .

MAT099 and CSE098 are prerequisites for this course. You must have a waiver or passing grade for both of these courses. Please indicate below which you have.

Course	Waiver		Passed		Quarter
MAT099	yes	no	yes	no	
CSE098	yes	no	yes	no	

Indicate by putting a "P" next to any of these Basic Skills courses which you have passed. Place an "R" next to any of these courses which are requirements for you, but you have not yet passed.

CSE096 ___	HUC098 ___	ENG098 ___	ESL096 ___
CSE097 ___	HUC099 ___	ENG099 ___	ESL097 ___
CSE098 ___			ESL098 ___
CSE099 ___	MAT098 ___		ESL099 ___
CSE103 ___	MAT099 ___		

B.   Practice Reading Activities

1.   Cloze Test. Below is a passage from your text. It
has some words missing. Fill in the blank spaces
with the words which you think the author of the
text used. Transfer your answers to the blanks
below and on page 7, and then count the number of
correct responses by checking with the correct
answers on page 8. This test is designed to
measure your reading ability. Do not be
discouraged if you get very few correct answers.

A rather complicated formula, beyond the scope of this

book, defines a normal distribution in terms of μ and σ,

the mean and standard deviation of the population

distribution. It is only through this formula that we can

verify if a distribution is normal. However, we can look

at the graph of a normal distribution and get a good

pictorial idea of some of the essential features of any

normal distribution. The graph of a 1_____

distribution is called a 2_____ curve. It possesses a

3_____ very much like the 4_____ section of a

pile 5_____ dry sand. Because of 6_____ shape

blacksmiths would sometimes 7_____ a pile of dry

8_____ in the construction of 9_____ mold for a

bell. 10_____ the normal curve is 11_____

called a bell-shaped 12_____ .

We see that a 13_____ normal curve is smooth

14_____ symmetrical about the vertical 15_____

over the mean μ. 16_____ that the highest point

17_____ the curve occurs over 18_____ . If the

distribution were 19_____ on a piece of 20_____

metal, cut out, and 21_____ on a knife edge,

22 _____ balance point would be 23 _____ μ. We

also see 24 _____ the curve tends to 25 _____ out

and approach the 26 _____ (x-axis) like a 27 _____

making a landing. However, 28 _____ mathematical

theory such a 29 _____ would never quite finish

30 _____ landing because a normal 31 _____ never

touches the horizontal 32 _____. The parameter σ

controls 33 _____ spread of the curve. 34 _____

curve is quite close 35 _____ the horizontal axis at

36 _____ and μ−3σ. Thus, if 37 _____ standard

deviation σ is 38 _____, the curve will be 39 _____

spread out; if it 40 _____ small, the curve will

41 _____ more peaked. The figure 42 _____ the

normal curve is 43 _____ downward for an interval

44 _____ either side of the 45 _____ μ. Then it

begins 46 _____ cup upward as we 47 _____ to the

lower part 48 _____ the bell. The exact 49 _____

where the transition between 50 _____ and downward

cupping occur 51 _____ above the points μ +σ

52 _____ μ−σ.

Let's summarize the important properties of a normal curve.

1. The curve is "bell shaped" with the highest point
    over the mean μ.

2. It is symmetrical about the vertical line through
    μ.

3. The curve approaches the horizontal axis but never
    touches or crosses it.

4. The transition points between cupping upward and
    cupping downward occur at μ +σ and μ− σ.

Answers for the Cloze Procedure.

1.	normal	21.	placed	41.	be
2.	normal	22.	the	42.	shows
3.	shape	23.	at	43.	cupped
4.	cross	24.	that	44.	on
5.	of	25.	level	45.	mean
6.	its	26.	horizontal	46.	to
7.	use	27.	glider	47.	go
8.	sand	28.	in	48.	of
9.	a	29.	glider	49.	places
10.	So	30.	its	50.	upward
11.	also	31.	curve	51.	are
12.	curve	32.	axis	52.	and
13.	general	33.	the		
14.	and	34.	The		
15.	line	35.	to		
16.	Notice	36.	$\mu+3\sigma$		
17.	of	37.	the		
18.	μ	38.	large		
19.	graphed	39.	more		
20.	sheet	40.	is		

2. Fry Readability Estimate of the Text. Three passages were selected from the textbook for readability analysis using the Fry Readability Estimate.

5.9	158	10
5.0	159	11
6.0	142	7

Means 5.6   153

Using the above means, the Fry Readability estimate was found to be at the 9.5 grade level.

Note: Students who have trouble with this course and who read below the 9th grade level may be helped by having their reading ability improved.

C. Practice Writing Activity

Writing Sample. In the space below write a few sentences which describe your worst experience in a mathematics class.

In the space below write a few sentences which describe your best experience in a mathematics class.

D. Practice Oral/Aural Activity

Breaking the Ice. Students will pair off. In turn each student will tell his partner his name, a few things about himself, and one thing which makes him unique or different. When this has been accomplished, each student will stand up, in turn, to introduce his partner to the class by stating his partner's name, a few things about him, and one thing which makes him unique.

E. Practice Mathematics Activity

Mathematical Skills Assessment.

1. Write the number .70 in the form of a percent.
2. Which is larger: 2.7 or 2.67?
3. Write the fraction 10/40 in the form of a percent.
4. Write the fraction 46/10 in the form of a decimal.
5. The number 3.7 is closest to which whole number?
6. Do this subtraction: (7) - (5).
7. Do this subtraction: (5) - (7).
8. Simplify: $\sqrt{25}$.
9. What number do you get when you square the number 12?
10. What is the average (mean) of the following numbers: 23.1, 20, 21.4, 25.3, 19.2?

III. COURSE REQUIREMENTS

A. Reading Requirements

1. Reading Assignments. For each class meeting there
is an assigned reading. In general, a reading
assignment consists of an entire section of the
textbook. Reading mathematics is a slow process.
You may have to read a phrase, sentence, or paragraph many times before its meaning becomes clear.
All reading assignments should be done with pencil
in hand and with an ample supply of paper.
Throughout the text there are illustrative examples
and exercises which you should work out yourself
(on paper) along with the author. The reading
assignments are listed in the Learning Guide on
page 4.

2. Guide Questions. There are reading guide questions
to assist you with each reading assignment. The
guide questions are to be answered in writing and
to be handed in with the homework. The purpose of
the guide questions is to help you focus on the
most important concepts in the assignment. The
guide questions are listed with the reading assignments which begin on page 19.

3. Vocabulary. Along with the guide questions, your
reading assignment will also contain a list of
words and symbols which are to be found in the
readings. In a binder with pages lettered alpha-
betically each student will be asked to record the
meanings of the items in this "vocabulary" list as
part of the reading assignment. This personal
dictionary will be a handy reference to the student
throughout the course and will be collected on the
last day of the course. Students are encouraged to
include in this personal dictionary any other
interesting words which you come across in other
courses or in your reading.

4. Previewing. The entire text and each chapter
individually will be previewed by the instructor
with the class. This will help prepare you for the
important features of the upcoming material.

B. Writing Requirements

1. Written Assignments. A group of problems from the
text are assigned for each day. These problems are
to be done on 8 1/2 by 11 inch paper and handed in
at the end of each class period. The written
responses to the reading guide questions are to be

included as well. The written assignments of problems can be found in the section which gives the daily assignments beginning on page 18.

2. <u>Ditto Preparation</u>. As part of each student's oral presentation of the homework (see page 12), he or she will be required to prepare a ditto master of the solutions to the homework problems and the guide questions.

3. <u>Brief Writing Assignments</u>. Written responses in prose form will be required on many of the tests given during the course. An example of the type of question is given below:

   <u>The Literary Digest Fiasco</u>

   Before the presidential election of 1936 the <u>Literary Digest</u> conducted a survey of telephone and <u>Digest</u> subscribers. They contacted 10 million people! Their results indicated that Alf Landon would win by a two-to-one landslide.

   Explain (give reason) why the sample used to make the prediction was not an appropriate one for predicting the results of a national election. Follow this explanation with an illustration (example) of how a modern magazine might choose a sample to predict the results of a national election.

   Two or three paragraphs should be sufficient to complete this assignment adequately.

4. <u>Research Project</u>. Each student will complete a research project during the course. The steps in the research project are described in the daily assignments. The first step in the research project is found on page 20.

   The project consists of seven pieces (steps) which will be due at various points throughout the course. For each step you will first write a draft. The draft should be proofread for grammar, punctuation, spelling, and sense. The instructor will read the draft of each step and comment on it. Use these comments to improve further drafts. When the draft of step 2 is due, you should include a revision of draft 1 as well. Thus your final paper will evolve from a series of improved drafts. Only the final document need by typed. It should be double spaced, with one-inch margins and in a binder. Any standard style guide may be used--the APA Style Guide is a good one and is available in the library.

   I will be concerned with grammatical as well as

mathematical errors. The due dates for each step are found on page 4. The final document is due on the last day of the course.

It will be the responsibility of the student to arrange an office visit with the instructor during either the second or third week of the course. It will be a short meeting during which your project will be discussed.

When any project report is returned to the student with the words "See me" writtten on it, it is the responsibility of the student to see the instructor in his office within one week of the receipt of such notice.

The final paper will receive a grade based on the following:

Writing	25%
Statistics	25%
Neatness	25%
Completeness	25%

C. Oral/Aural Requirements

1. Listening Activity. The instructor will randomly select one student at the end of each class to hand in his or her notes for the day. The instructor will go with the student to the math office where the notes will be xeroxed and the originals returned to the student.

   The copy will be examined by the instructor for a demonstration of the ability to record the important ideas and examples in an accurate and organized way. The copy will be returned to the student at the next class meeting with comments and appropriate referrals if necessary.

   Besides enabling the instructor to determine how well communication is taking place, this activity will help the instructor monitor his own organization of his classroom presentation--so that good note-taking is a possibility. By spreading this activity over the entire quarter, this may also have the effect of keeping the students more active in the learning process.

2. Oral Activity. At the first class meeting each student will be assigned a day on which he or she will be responsible for that day's homework. That means the student must prepare the solution to all of the homework problems and he will be asked to get up in front of the class and thoroughly explain how to solve at least one of the problems.

a. Purposes

(1)   To provide the student with the opportunity to speak before a group.

(2)   To encourage the student to strive for a deeper level of understanding of the concepts in the course. This deeper understanding is necessary for teaching concepts, while it is not necessarily needed for the reception of the information.

(3)   To have the class hear another (different?) explanation of the concepts and techniques involved in the homework assignment.

(4)   To create a solution set of all the homework assignments for the students.

b. Guidelines

Preparation

(1)   Understand the concepts presented in the course. Don't let the instructor go on to new techniques and topics when you are not following!

(2)   Get in the habit of speaking the language of mathematics (statistics) by discussing the solutions of your homework problems with your classmates or by doing homework together.

(3)   Read ahead in the book, especially as the date of your presentation nears. Read about the upcoming topics in the references which have been put on reserve in the library.

(4)   See if you can start to make progress on your assigned problems even before the method of attacking them has been covered in class.

(5)   A few days before the assignment is due, obtain the following items from the instructor:

      (a) transparencies
      (b) pens for the tranparencies
      (c) ditto masters

(6)   Do the assignment as usual on paper to be

handed in. When you are satisfied with your solutions, transfer them to the transparencies (write clearly and large) and also to the ditto masters--don't forget to pull out the protective paper from the ditto master before you start to write and replace it when you are finished. Peek inside the ditto master to see if you're pressing hard enough. Don't get excited if it looks like mirror writing in there!

(7) Practice aloud by explaining your solutions to other students.

(8) The ditto masters should be given to the instructor for reproduction at least 30 minutes before class.

c. Presentation

(1) Be early for class to "set up."

(2) Test the overhead projector to see if it's positioned properly.

(3) Place the ditto sheets near the door so that the students may pick them up as they enter.

(4) The instructor will choose (or ask the class to choose) a problem for you to solve.

(5) You will place the solution to that problem on the overhead. You will then go through the step-by-step procedures which you used to reach the solution. During this presentation you may refer to the worked-out solution on the overhead and may use the blackboard. Don't forget to include in your presentation:

(a) what is given
(b) what is your goal
(c) the strategies to be used
(d) all the steps in the solution
(e) methods of checking

(6) Assume that the students in the class have not been exposed to the concepts and techniques which you employ in the solution of the problem. Explain these thoroughly. Teach your classmates!

(7) Be prepared to stop at any time during your presentation for questions from

either the students or the instructor.

(8) You may be asked to present more than one of the homework problems.

(9) Remember these suggestions for good "teaching." Face the class when working at the overhead projector, and try to maintain as much eye contact as possible with the students. Don't focus on the instructor--he already knows how to do the problems! When working on the board, don't talk while facing the board. Turn around to talk. If you forget what to do next or don't know the answer to a question, ask one of the other students to make a suggestion.

d. Grading Your Presentation

The instructor will grade your presentation based on the following breakdown.

Quality of the transparencies and dittos....50%
Clear presentation of the solution(s).......40%
Ability to respond to questions.............10%
Bonus points will be awarded for the following:
  Analogies drawn
  Generalizations made
  Good questions posed
  Interesting alternative solutions suggested
  Good examples (or counterexamples) offered
  Evidence of insight or innovation
  Construction of physical models for
    demonstration
  Evidence of the use of the books on reserve

Name _____ Score _____

Feedback Form

1. <u>Quality of the Transparencies and Dittos</u>   50%

    Are they complete, neat, and organized well?

---

2. <u>Clear Presentation of the Solution</u>   40%

    Did you demonstrate a thorough understanding of the
    techniques and concepts involved? Did you present the
    solution(s) in a clear step-by-step manner? Also
    considered in this section are the use of verbal
    fillers, volume, pace, and grammar.

---

3. <u>Ability to Respond to Questions</u>   10%

    Did you seem to anticipate the questions? Did you help
    the questioner clarify or solve his or her problem?

<u>Bonus Points</u>

e. Reacting to Students' Responses in Class

(1) List of Behaviors to Be Corrected

Answering a "different" question
Grammatical error
Mispronunciation
Misenunciation
Lack of eye contact
Poor volume
Monotone
Poor logic
Misuse of words
Annoying fillers

(2) List of Behaviors to Be Applauded

The "opposites" of the above
Answering a question (giving a solution)
    in more than one way
Employing problem-solving heuristics
Evidence of reading the text or references

(3) Attending to Oral Skills

When the oral assignment is first given to
the class, the instructor will list--and
provide examples of--the types of behavior
which should be avoided (sought).

The method of correction will either be
immediate and particular or periodic and
general. Errors in content will usually
require immediate attention, whereas
errors in form will most often be handled
in summary remarks about student behavior
in general.

D. Mathematics

At the beginning of appropriate chapters, students will
be asked to solve a set of mathematics problems which
are prerequisite to the mathematical concepts embedded
in the statistical content of the chapter. Students
who demonstrate a lack of sufficient understanding of
these prerequisite mathematical skills will be assigned
extra drill sheets in their area of weakness and/or
will be asked to attend the Mathematics Lab for
remediation.

IV. GRADING AND SEATING

A. Grading

Your grade will be computed according to the following distribution:

Chapter Tests   30%
Final Exam   40%
Research Report   15%
Other Assignments 15%*

*Homework, class participation, oral/aural assignments, etc.

B. Seating Arrangement

Students will sit in the standard arrangement. At times the students will be asked to work in groups on worksheets. When this occurs, some students will turn their chairs to face others in groups of 3 or 4.

V. ASSIGNMENTS AND MATERIALS

A. Explanation

The rest of the learning guide contains the assignments and materials which you will need for each day's work. Each of the daily assignments and materils will include one or more of the following items:

Vocabulary Items, Reading Guide Questions, and Assigned Problems from the Text

Directions for Steps in the Research Report

Math Prerequisite Skills for the Chapter

Worksheets to Be Used in Class

Sample End-of-Chapter Tests

Note: For meeting #2 (pp. 19-20) there are vocabulary items, reading guide questions, and assigned problems. Also included are the mathematics prerequisites for chapters 1 and 2. For meeting #3 (pp. 20-21) there are vocabulary items, reading guide questions, and assigned problems. Also included is step 1 of the research report. For meeting #4 (pp. 22) vocabulary items,

reading guide questions, and assigned problems
from the text; worksheets to be used in class;
and sample end-of-chapter tests are included.

B. Assignments and Materials for Each Meeting

For Meeting #2 (pp. 9-15)

Vocabulary Items, Reading Guide Questions, and Assigned
Problems from the Text

Define the following words using two different sources:
the text or any of the books on reserve in the library
and a standard dictionary.

random	datum	statistics
sample	data	simulation
population	statistic	phenomena

1. Give an example of a population.

2. Give an example of a sample from the population in
question 2.

3. How should the ranchers (p. 11) have attacked and
solved the Coyote-Sheep problem?

4. Give a specific example of how random numbers could
be used to simulate a particular phenomenon other
than those used in the text.

5. Do problems 1, 3, 5, 7, and 9 on pages 14 and 15.

Mathematics Prerequisites for Chapters 1 and 2

1. What is 30% of 2,000,000?

2. Write 0.20 as a percent and as a fraction.

3. Write 15% as a decimal and as a fraction.

4. Write 39/5 as a decimal rounded off to the nearest
whole number.

5. Write in words 2.5 (don't use the word "point").

6. What is the difference between 0.5% and 0.13%?

7. Which is larger, 0.08 or 0.1?

8. Add 2.48, 3.5, and 1.8.

9. How many degrees are there in one revolution?

10. How many degrees are there in 7/9 of a revolution?

11. Simplify: $\dfrac{48 - 6}{3}$

12. Simplify: $\dfrac{8 + 13}{2}$

13. Simplify: 18 + 0.05

14. Simplify: 18 - 0.05

For Meeting #3 (pp. 16-24)

Vocabulary Items, Reading Guide Questions, and Assigned Problems from the Text

Add the following to your vocabulary list:

pictogram   table   vertical

circle graph   chronological   horizontal

graph   trend   ⎯⋀⎯⎯

uniformly   bar graph   axis

1. Construct a bar graph for table 2-1 (p. 16).

2. Construct a bar graph for table 2-2 (p. 17).

3. Explain why the graphs for #2 and #3 are different.

4. Estimate the effective temperature from figure 2-6 (p. 17).

5. Do problems 1, 2, 3, 4, and 6 on page 23ff.

Directions for Steps in the Research Report

Step 1--Method of Data Collection

1. Describe your target population for this project.

2. What size sample are you planning to use? (minimum: n = 30).

3. Describe (give details) how you intend to select the subjects in your sample.

4. Will your sample be random? Explain why (not).

5. The questionnaire which you develop for this
    project must contain six questions. Three of these
    should be "number generators" and three should be
    "category fillers."

    Number Generators: How many . . . do you have?
                         How many times a month do
                             you . . .?
                         How much money . . .?

    Category Fillers: Are you A or B?
                         Do you prefer . . ., . . .,
                             or . . .?
                         Do you . . .? Yes or no.

    Number Generators:

        1.

        2.

        3.

    Category Fillers:

        1. (two possible responses)

        2. (two possible responses)

        3. (three possible responses)

6. Do you think that higher scores on any number
    generator question will be useful in predicting the
    type of response to any other number generating
    question? If so, state the relationship
    hypothesized.

    (For example, higher scores on "How much do you
    spend on candy each week?" should indicate higher
    scores on "How much do you weigh?")

7. Do you think that any of the category filler
    questions are related? If so, state the
    hypothesized relationship.

    (For example, "Do you spend more than 3 nights a
    week dating?" and "Is your GPA higher than 2.0?"
    should be related.)

8. For each of the number generating questions,
    predict your estimate of the mean of the responses.

    (For example, the mean response to the question,
    "How many siblings do you have?" will be 1.5.)

For Meeting #4 (pp. 24-34)

<u>Vocabulary Items, Reading Guide Questions, and Assigned
Problems from the Text</u>

Add the following to your vocabulary list:

histogram	class	class width
assimilation	lower class limit	midpoint of a class
$\approx$	upper class limit	frequency table
tally	continuous	polygon
class boundaries	frequency polygon	

1. In figure 2-12 why do you think that they are using decimals on the age axis?

2. What is the class width in figure 2-14?

3. What is the midpoint of the first interval in figure 2-14?

4. What are the class boundaries of the first interval in figure 2-14?

5. What is the relationship of a frequency polygon and a histogram?

6. Do 1, 2, 3, and 4 on page 32.

Worksheet for Section 2-3

Largest Data Value =

Smallest Data Value =

Range = Largest - Smallest =

# of Classes Desired = C =

Class Width = Range/C =   (Round up to the nearest
                                unit)

Midpoint Width = (Upper Limit - Lower Limit)/2

Class Width = Upper Boundary - Lower Boundary

Class Lower Limit	–	Class Upper Limit	Class Lower Boundary	–	Class Upper Boundary	Tally	f	Mid-point
	–			–				
	–			–				
	–			–				
	–			–				
	–			–				

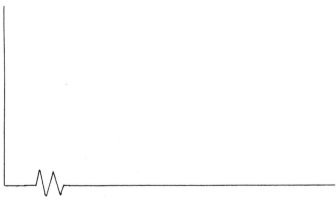

Histogram

Sample Chapter Tests

SAMPLE CHAPTER TEST 1*

1. In your own words give a definition of the terms "population" and "sample."

2. The phone company in Chicago wants to estimate the number of calls made from home phones in Chicago. Five hundred home-phone owners were asked to keep careful records of the number of calls made per week.

    (a) What is the population?
    (b) What is the sample?

3. A sociologist in Los Angeles wants to know the number of hours a ten-year-old child in Los Angeles watches TV each day. A group of 100 ten-year-olds in Los Angeles are selected at random and asked how many hours they watch TV each day.

    (a) What is the population?
    (b) What is the sample?

SAMPLE CHAPTER TEST 2*

1. The principal gases that compose the earth's atmosphere are nitrogen, 78.1%; oxygen, 21.0%; and argon, 0.9%. Make a circle graph representing this information.

2. Use a random number table to simulate 20 throws of a fair die. Explain your method of simulation and use of the random number table.

3. The length of time (in months) between the onset of a type of malaria and its recurrence was recorded for 40 patients. The results follow:

4	6	18	6	19	6	7	2	4	6
2	4	10	7	7	9	5	4	4	5
5	8	7	8	9	13	11	13	16	11
10	14	11	13	9	7	8	19	7	8

    a. Make a frequency table using lower class limits 2, 4, 6, 8, 10, 12, 16, and 18.

    b. Make a histogram and identify the class midpoints.

    c. Make a frequency polygon.

*From Test Program and Key Steps to Solutions for Even-Numbered Problems by Charles Henry Brase and Corrine Pellillo Brase (Material published in conjunction with Understandable Statistics) Copyright © 1978 by D.C. Heath and Company. Reprinted by permission.

For Meeting #5 (pp. 39-47)

Vocabulary Items, Reading Guide Questions, and Assigned
Problems from the Text

Add the following to your vocabulary list:

average	median	sigma
mean	Σ	Σx
mode	$\bar{x}$	n

1. Do extreme scores in a distribution have a greater
   effect on the mean or the median (see example 4
   p. 45)?

2. Explain how you calculate the mean, mode, and
   median of a distribution of 5 scores.

3. Verify that the mean, mode, and median of -1, 0, 1,
   2, 2, 2 are 1, 2, and 1.5, respectively.

4. Do problems 1, 4, 5, and 6 on page 46.

Additional Mathematics Prerequisites for Chapter 3

1. Simplify:

   (a) $8 - 6$
   (b) $6 - 8$
   (c) $(9 - 2)^2$
   (d) $(2 - 9)^2$

2. Find the mean of the following scores: 3, 5, 7, 2,
   and 0.

3. Find the following by using a calculator or the
   square root table in the text.

   (a) $\sqrt{9}$

   (b) $\sqrt{28}$

   (c) $\sqrt{280}$

   (d) $\sqrt{2.83}$

4. If n stands for 6, what does n-1 stand for?

5. If $s^2 = 7.36$, find $\sqrt{s^2}$.

Worksheet for Section 3-1

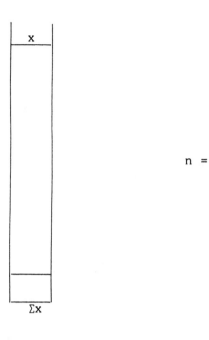

n =

mean $\bar{x} = \Sigma x/n$

mode (most frequent) =

median (middle) =

For Meeting #6 (pp. 48-54)

Vocabulary Items, Reading Guide Questions, and Assigned Problems from the Text

Add the following to your vocabulary list:

cross reference s^2 standard deviation

variance $\sqrt{}$ s

range $\sqrt{variance}$ $x - \bar{x}$

deviation percentile rank $(x - \bar{x})^2$

$$\sqrt{\frac{\Sigma (x - \bar{x})^2}{n - 1}}$$

1. Although each of the following distributions have the same mean (50), which seems more spread out?

     (a) 1, 2, 50, 98, 99
     (b)   48, 49, 50, 51, 52

2. Compare what is measured by a variation and by an average.

3. Create a distribution with a mean of 0 and a standard deviation of 0.

4. Create a distribution with a mean of 10 and a standard deviation of 0.

5. Create a distribution with a mean of 10 and a range of 0.

6. Create a distribution with a mean of 0 and a range of 0.

7. Find the square root of 38 using the table in the text.

8. Do problems 2 and 5 on page 53 ff.

Directions for Steps in the Research Report

Step 2--Organization of the Data

1. Collect the data from each subject in your sample. Record the raw data by subject.

2. For each of the questions on your questionnaire, do the following:

    (a) List the raw data.

    (b) Organize the data into the form of at least two of the following:

             a table
             a bar graph
             a circle graph
             a pictogram
             a histogram
             a frequency polygon

    Note: Each of these 6 forms must be used at least once.

Worksheet for Section 3-2

n =

x	x − $\bar{x}$	$(x - \bar{x})^2$
Σx =	0 ✓	

$\bar{x} = \Sigma x/n$

$$s = \sqrt{\frac{(x - \bar{x})^2}{n - 1}}$$

For Meeting #7 (pp. 54-63)

<u>Vocabulary Items, Reading Guide Questions, and Assigned
Problems from the Text</u>

Add the following to your vocabulary list:

x

xf

$\Sigma x f$

$\dfrac{\Sigma x f}{n}$

$$\sqrt{\dfrac{\Sigma (x - \bar{x})^2 f}{n - 1}}$$

1. What is the advantage of using grouped data?

2. Make sure you work through example 4 (p. 56) before
   you do problems 1 and 3 on page 58.

Worksheet for Section 3-3

Class	f	x	xf	$x - \bar{x}$	$(x - \bar{x})^2$	$(x - \bar{x})^2 f$
	$n\checkmark$					

$$\bar{x} = \Sigma xf/n$$

$$s = \sqrt{\frac{\Sigma(x - \bar{x})^2 f}{n - 1}}$$

For Meeting #8 (reread pp. 54-63)

Assigned problem:

1. Do #2 on page 58.

SAMPLE CHAPTER TEST 3*

1. A company that sells frozen crab legs prints
    "contents 14 oz" on each package. A random sample
    of five packages showed the contents to weigh, in
    ounces,

    13.6   13.7   14.0   14.4   13.6

    (a) Find the mean, median, and mode.
    (b) Find the range and sample standard deviation.

2. The manager of the Westside Apartment Complex
    interviewed 25 families who wanted to rent
    apartments. The following data on family size was
    obtained:

No. of people in family	2	3	4	5	6	7
No. of families with this many members	3	10	5	2	4	1

    (a) Find the mean numbers of people per family.
    (b) Find the sample standard deviation.

For Meeting #9 (pp. 64-69)

Vocabulary Items, Reading Guide Questions, and Assigned
Problems from the Text

Add the following to your vocabulary list:

P(A)	equally likely	relative frequency
probability	outcomes	f/n
intuition	sample space	probability of an event

1. What are the three ways of determining the
    probability of an event?

2. Can P(A) be greater than 100%?

3. Can P(A) be less than 0?

4. If P(A) = 0, then what can you say about A?

5. Do 1, 2, 3, 5, and 7 on page 69.

Additional Mathematics Prerequisites for Chapter 4

1. 5! = (5) (4) (3) (2) (1) = ?

2. 3/5 times 4/5 = ?

3. 21/25 times 20/24 = ?

4. 4/52 + 13/52 - 1/52 = ?

5. 5/17 + 3/17 = ?

6. Add 0.8 + 0.46 + 0.021

7. Simplify: $(3.4)^2$ 5

For Meeting #10 (pp. 71-79)

Vocabulary Items, Reading Guide Questions, and Assigned Problems from the Text

Add the following to your vocabulary list:

dependent	dependent events	mutually
independent	independent events	exclusive
P(A and B)	P(A or B)	mutually
		exclusive events
discrete		

1. How many cards in a bridge deck are
    a. jacks and diamonds?
    b. jacks or diamonds?

2. Why does the independence of events matter in determining probabilities?

3. If there are 4 aces in the deck and 13 spades in the deck, why are there only 16 cards which are either aces or spades?

4. Do 1, 3, 6, and 7 on page 80.

For Meeting #11 (pp. 81-89)

Vocabulary Items, Reading Guide Questions, and Assigned
Problems from the Text

Add the following to your vocabulary list:

random variable   μ

continuous   σ

probability distribution   parameters

expected value of a
probability distribution

1. What is the area under the histograms in figure
    4-7?

2. What is the difference between a parameter and a
    statistic?

3. Do 1 and 2 on page 88.

Worksheet for Section 4-3

x	f	P(x)

x	P(x)	xP(x)	x - μ	$(x - μ)^2$	$(x - μ)^2 P(x)$

$$\mu = \Sigma x P(x) \qquad \qquad \sigma = \sqrt{(x - \mu)^2 P(x)}$$

For Meeting #12 (reread pp. 81-89)

Assigned problems:

1. Do 3 and 5 on page 89.

Directions for Steps in the Research Report

Step 3--Statistical Description of the Data

1. For each of the number-generating questions, give the following statistics:

    a. n   d. median

    b. $\bar{x}$ e. range

    c. mode   f. s

SAMPLE CHAPTER TEST 4*

1. Mario commissions his paintings to be sold in a gallery in Estes Park. The gallery clerk kept an inventory list of the number of Mario paintings sold each day for 120 days.

x, number of Mario paintings sold per day	f, number of days this many Mario paintings were sold
0	9
1	20
2	45
3	24
4	25
5	7

   a. If a day is chosen at random from the 120 observed days, what is the probability that x equals 0? 1? 2? 3? 4? 5?

   b. Is x a continuous or discrete random variable?

   c. Graph the probability distribution for x.

   d. If a day is chosen at random, what is the probability that three or more Mario paintings were sold?

   e. What is the expected value for the number of Mario paintings sold per day?

   f. What is the standard deviation of the x distribution?

2. Two teams are climbing Mount Everest independently.
    The leader of Team A believes their chances of
    reaching the summit are 0.70, and the leader of
    Team B believes their chances are 0.85.

    a. What is the probability both teams reach the
        summit?
    b. What is the probability at least one team
        reaches the summit?
    c. What is the probability neither team reaches
        the summit?

3. A Marine captain asks for two volunteers to perform
    a dangerous mission. Six Marines step forward.
    Among them are two close friends, George and
    Howard, who want to perform the mission.
    The captain first chooses one man at random and
    then randomly chooses the second from the remaining
    volunteers.

    a. What is the probability that George is chosen,
        given Howard has already been chosen?
    b. What is the probability that both George and
        Howard are chosen?
    c. What is the probability George and Howard do
        not form the team sent on the mission?

For Meeting #13 (pp. 249-256)

Vocabulary Items, Reading Guide Questions, and Assigned
Problems from the Text

Add the following to your vocabulary list:

paired data	simultaneously	linear
correlation	regression	linear correlation
scatter		

1. Is there a correlation between smoking and cancer?
    Explain.

2. Is there a correlation between age and height of
    teenage boys? Is it positive or negative?

3. Does the scattergram in example 2 on page 354
    indicate a positive or negative correlation?

4. What does negative correlation mean?

5. Do 1, 2, 3, 4, 5, 6, and 7 on page 255.

Additional Mathematics Prerequisites for Chapters 9 and 5

1. Complete the table in order to find the items listed below:

x	x^2
1	
2	
3	
4	

$$\Sigma x =$$

$$(\Sigma x)^2 =$$

$$\Sigma x^2 =$$

2. Simplify: $\dfrac{842}{\sqrt{247}\ \sqrt{83}}$

3. $1 - 3/7 =$

4. If $p = 1/3$, $q = 2/3$, $n = 4$, and $r = 1$,

   find the value of $p^t\ q^{n-r}$.

5. Simplify: $\dfrac{6!}{4!\ (6 - 4)!}$

6. Simplify: $\sqrt{6(0.5)\ (0.5)}$

For Meeting #14 (pp. 269-280)

Vocabulary Items, Reading Guide Questions, and Assigned Problems from the Text

Add the following to your vocabulary list:

correlation coefficient   zero correlation

s_x Σxy

r   negligible

positive correlation x^2

negative correlation $(\Sigma x)^2$

1. Draw a scattergram showing a zero correlation.

2. Draw a scattergram showing a high positive
    correlation.

3. Draw a scattergram showing a strong negative
    linear correlation.

4. How does the author get $\sqrt{24891} \simeq 157.77$ on the
    bottom of page 275?

5. Do 1, 3, and 5 on page 279.

Worksheet for Section 9-3

x	y	x^2	y^2	xy

$\Sigma\,x\ =$

$\Sigma\,y\ =$

$$r = \frac{n(\Sigma\,xy)\ -\ (\Sigma\,x)\ (\Sigma\,y)}{\sqrt{n(\Sigma\,x^2)\ -\ (\Sigma\,x)^2}\ \ \sqrt{n(\Sigma\,y^2)\ -\ (\Sigma\,y)^2}}$$

$\Sigma\,x^2\ =$

$\Sigma\,y^2\ =$

$\Sigma\,xy\ =$

$n\ =$

$(\Sigma\,x)^2\ =$

$(\Sigma\,y)^2\ =$

For Meeting #15 (reread pp. 269-280)

Assigned problems:

1. Do 2 and 4 on page 279.

SAMPLE CHAPTER TEST 9*

1. A psychology instructor tells students that there
    is a correlation between the length of time spent
    to complete a multiple choice exam and the score
    on the exam. The instructor uses the following
    data:

x (time, min)	15	20	25	35	45
y (score)	80	100	80	90	60

    a. Draw a scatter diagram. If there is a
        correlation, does the scatter diagram indicate
        positive or negative correlation?
    b. Compute r.

For Meeting #16 (pp. 95-100)

Vocabulary Items, Reading Guide Questions, and Assigned
Problems from the Text

Add the following to your vocabulary list:

binomial   q   p + q

binomial experiment   1 - p   with replacement

p   1 - q   without replacement

1. Give an example (not in the text) of a binomial
    experiment.

2. Why is your example in #1 a binomial experiment?

3. For a trial of a binomial experiment p = 1/3. What
    is the value of q?

4. Do 1, 3, 5, and 6 on page 100.

For Meeting #17 (pp. 101-106)

Vocabulary Items, Reading Guide Questions, and Assigned Problems from the Text

Add the following to your vocabulary list:

$C_{n,r}$ $\qquad$ $P(r)$ $\qquad$ $C_{4,3}$

$C_{n,r} p^r q^{n-r}$ $\qquad$ $\dfrac{n!}{r! \ (n-r)!}$ $\qquad$ $r > 4$

binomial coefficient $\qquad\qquad\qquad\qquad$ $r \leq 4$

1. Verify that $C_{8,3} = 56$ from the table of binomial coefficients on page 313.

2. Write each of the following using inequality symbols:

    a. r is greater than 5
    b. r is less than or equal to 5
    c. r is at least 5
    d. r is at most 5
    e. r is 3 or less
    f. r is 2 or more

3. Do 1, 3, 5, and 7 on page 106.

Directions for Steps in the Research Report

Step 4--Correlation Coefficient

1. Choose two of the number-generating questions which you think are related in some way. Refer to #6 of step 1 for such a hypothesized relationship. State these questions.

    X:

    Y:

2. Make a scattergram for the (x,y) data.

3. Estimate the strength of the relationship between x and y by looking at the scattergram. Do you think that r will be closest to -1, 0, or +1?

4. Complete a table like the following for the data.

x	y	x^2	y^2	xy
Σx	Σy	Σx^2	Σy^2	Σxy

5. Now compute $(\Sigma x)^2$ and $(\Sigma y)^2$.

6. Finally, compute r using the formula on page 272.

7. Using the computed value of r and the table on page 278, describe the strength of the relationship of the variables under question.

Worksheet for Section 5-2

Binomial Experiment:

One Trial   Outcomes:
$$\text{Success} =$$
$$\text{Failure} =$$

p = probability of success =

q = probability of failure =

n Trials

Number of successes = r =

$n - r =$

$$C_{n,r} = \frac{n!}{r! \, (n - r)!} =$$

$$P(r) = C_{n,r} p^{r} q^{n-r} =$$

For Meeting #18 (pp. 107-113)

<u>Vocabulary Items, Reading Guide Questions, and Assigned</u>
<u>Problems from the Text</u>

Add the following to your vocabulary list:

area	symmetrical
round-off error	np
skewed	$\sqrt{npq}$
skewed to the left	n factorial
skewed to the right	n!
coincide	

1. Why is a histogram an appropriate graph for a binomial distribution?

2. What is the area under the histogram in figure 5-1?

3. Complete exercise 6 on page 109.

4. Do 1 and 2 on page 113 and 2, 4, and 9 on page 106.

Worksheet for Section 5-3

Binomial Experiment:

One Trial   Outcomes: Success =

                               Failure =

                        p =

                        q =

r	P(r)

Note: the mean number of
        successes expected
        in n trials is given
        by

$$\mu = np$$

        the standard deviation
        of the number of successes
        in n trials is given by

$$\sigma = \sqrt{npq}$$

P(r)

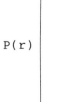

r

For Meeting #19 (reread pp. 107-113)

Assigned problems:

1. Do 3 and 5 on page 114.

SAMPLE CHAPTER TEST 5*

1. The Davy Jones Scuba Gear Company makes tank
   regulators. On the average, one out of five
   regulators is defective. Let r be the number of
   defective regulators in a random sample of seven
   Davy Jones regulators.

   a. Find P(r) for r = 0, 1, 2, 3, 4, 5, 6, and 7.

   b. Make a histogram for the r probability
      distribution.

   c. What is the expected number of defective
      regulators in a sample of size seven?

   d. What is the standard deviation of the
      probability distribution in problem 1?

   e. What is the probability that none of the seven
      are defective? What is the probability that at
      least one is defective?

For Meeting #20 (pp. 291-302)

Vocabulary Items, Reading Guide Questions, and Assigned
Problems from the Text

Add the following to your vocabulary list:

Chi	contingency table	$(0 - E)^2$
χ^2	rows	$\Sigma \dfrac{(0 - E)^2}{E}$
d.f.	columns	
cells	observed frequency	$(R - 1)(C - 1)$
contingency	expected frequency	$\chi^2 \alpha$

1. Would you say that ability to bowl well and ability
   to shoot foul shots (basketball) well are
   independent? Explain.

2. Would you say that hair color and eye color on a
   person are independent? Explain.

3. Would you say that IQ and good looks are
    independent? Explain.

4. Complete the table in exercise 3 on page 297.

5. Do 1, 2, and 3 on page 301.

Additional Mathematics Prerequisites for Chapters 10,
6, and 8

1. Simplify: $(4 - 1)(7 - 1)$

2. 80/300 times 90/300 times 300 = ?

3. $\dfrac{80 \cdot 150}{300}$ = ?

4. If O stands for 30 and E stands for 40, what does
    the following stand for?

$$(O - E)^2$$

5. If m = 50 and s = 10, then m + 3s = ? and
    m − 3s = ?

6. $1 - 0.5$ = ?

7. $100\% - 95\%$ = ?

8. $\dfrac{7.8 - 2}{0.5}$ = ?

9. $\dfrac{12 - 15}{6}$ = ?

10. $0.7(-2) + 7$ = ?

11. $\dfrac{300}{\sqrt{25}}$ = ?

12. If $\bar{x} = m + z\dfrac{s}{\sqrt{n}}$ and if m = 2.7, z = 0.4, s = 18,

     and n = 36, find the value of $\bar{x}$.

Worksheet for Section 10-1

Contingency
Table

			Row Totals
0 = E =	0 = E =		
0 = E =	0 = E =		
Column Totals			n =

$$E = \frac{(Row\ Total)\ (Column\ Total)}{Sample\ Size}$$

Cell #	0	E	0 - E	$(0 - E)^2$	$(0 - E)^2/E$
			$0 \checkmark$		$\chi^2 =$

d.f. = (R - 1)(C - 1) =

$\alpha = 0.05$ χ^2 critical =

H_0 :

H_1 :

Is χ^2 larger than χ^2 critical? Yes: Reject H_0

No: Don't Reject H_0

SAMPLE CHAPTER TEST 10*

1. The Ready Drug Stores are doing a study about gross
    sales and summer weather conditions. A random
    sample of 250 summer days from Ready Drug Store
    locations all over the United States gave the
    following information:

Weather	Gross Sales (in Dollars)			
	Under 5,000	5,000-10,000	Over 10,000	
Clear	20	35	40	95
Rainy	12	68	75	155
	32	103	115	250

Use a chi-square test to determine if gross sales
and weather conditions are independent at the 0.05
level of significance.

Note: Assignments and materials for each of the 30
       class meetings were included in the Learning
       Guide for the students. However, only those
       assignments and materials for lessons 1
       through 20 are included here because of
       space considerations.

---

*From Test Program and Key Steps to Solutions for Even-Numbered Problems by
Charles Henry Brase and Corrine Pellillo Brase (Material published in con-
junction with Understandable Statistics) Copyright © 1978 by D.C. Heath and
Company. Reprinted by permission.

Supplemental Materials for

A LEARNING GUIDE FOR ELEMENTARY STATISTICS

For Instructor's Use

(not to be given to students)

Contents

I. READING

A. Previewing the Text

Important Features	Page	Concept to Be Introduced
1. Title	iii	Definition of statistics
2. Preface	vii	Definition of previewing
3. Table of Prerequisite Material	ix	Cumulative nature of Mathematics
4. Table of Contents	xiii	Design of the course
5. Examples	3	How to study a math book
6. Exercises	3	How to study a math book
7. Summary	6	Read it first!
8. Important Words & Symbols	6	Read this first!
9. Chapter Problems	6	Spiral approach is used
10. Introductory Material	2	Motivational
11. Numbering System	10	Section 2.1
12. Section Problems	14	Hay que practicar!
13. Tables in the Textual Material	18	Referral from the text
14. Tables in the Appendices	335	Demonstrate use of the square root table
15. Answers to the Odd-Numbered Problems	357	How does one do homework?
16. Prerequisite Sections for Chapter Problems	383	How does one do homework?
17. Index	387	Using the library as a resource

A. Previewing the Text

Script

1. What good can result from your study of statistics? Can anyone suggest an example of an application of statistics? Can anyone suggest a definition of "statistics"?

2. How come this book costs so much money? What are prefaces for? What do the words "overview" and "preview" mean?

3. How many absences are ok in this class? Why can't we miss a class? What do you do if you miss a class? (Exchange phone numbers at this point.) Why do people hate math? Can you like something which you constantly fail?

4. Here's what we're going to do in this course. We'll cover parts of every chapter except chapter 7. Chapter 1 is an introduction to the subject; chapter 2 provides techniques on methods of organizing information; 3 tells us how to summarize information; 4 gives us the mathematical theory we need to proceed further; 5 gives us a method of analyzing the results of two-outcome games; 6 gives a method of analyzing many-outcome games; 7 we skip; 8 shows us the power of this tool (statistics); 9 provides a method of telling if two things are related; 10.1 gives a method of testing whether two things are unrelated.

5. How do you read (study) a math book? How does this differ from the way you read a novel? How can you use the examples to help you?

6. What is the difference between an example and an exercise?

7. You may want to read this before you start the chapter. Why? Why does the author have it at the end of the chapter?

8. Would it be good to read this part first as well? Why? Can the dictionary help you? is there such a thing as a math dictionary?

9. How should the section problems be used to help learn this subject? How should I use the answer key (appendix 2)?

10. The chapter problems use a spiral approach. What does this mean? What good are more problems? What is appendix 3 used for?

11. What is the purpose of the introductory material at the beginning of each chapter?

12. What numbering system is used in this text?

13. People have done a lot of the work for us--look at the tables in the back of the book. How would you find $\sqrt{4}$ and the $\sqrt{40}$ by using the square root table? Can a calculator do that any better? Are calculators allowed? What features should one look for in buying a calculator?

14. What do you do when you reach a topic which you find difficult to understand after reading the Brases and listening to Giangrasso? Besides seeing the teacher, fellow students, and the lab tutors, what else is there? How do you know if a library book might be of help?

15. Figures (also referred to as tables) are used throughout the text. How do you interpret these? How do you know to what part of the text these figures refer?

B. Previewing the Chapters

Previewing Chapter 2

Important Features	Page	Concept to Be Introduced
1. Title	9	Definition of data
2. Introductory Material	10	Population vs. sample
3. Section Title	10	What is a random sample?
4. Numbering System	10	Design of text
5. Example	12	How do you study?
6. Exercise	13	How do you study?
7. Section Problems	23	Homework counts!
8. Chapter Problems	35	Tests will look like these
9. Summary	34	Minimum expected of you
10. Important Words & Symbols	34	Be able to define these
11. Tables in the Textual Material	14	What do you look at first in a table?
12. Answers to the Odd-Numbered Problems	357	How do you use the answers?

Important Features	Page	Concept to Be Introduced
13. Prerequisite Material	ix	Chapter 1
14. Prerequisite Sections for the Chapter Problems	383	Aid to homework
15. Random Number Table	342	What is it?

Script

1. What is a datum? And why would you want to organize data? Who organizes data?

2. Make a statement about people who smoke (cigarettes). How sure are you that the statement is correct? How would you prove it?

3. How would you get a fair cross-section of people in the country?

4. Why is this section called 2.1?

5. What is the difference between examples, exercises, section problems, and chapter problems?

6. Each quiz will include definitions from the Important Words & Symbols section.

7. What does the table on page 21 mean?

8. Where can you find the answers to the assignment?

9. Do you have to know what's in chapter 1 to be able to understand chapter 2? Why?

10. How do you use the information in appendix 3?

11. What is the table of random numbers? How was it formed?

Previewing Chapter 3

Important Features	Page	Concept to Be Introduced
1. Title	39	Definition of average and variation
2. Introductory Material	40	Intuitive average
3. Section Title	40	Definition of averages

Important Features	Page	Concept to Be Introduced
4. Section Title	54	Methods of organizing data
5. Prerequisite Material	ix	Chapters 1 and 2

Previewing Chapter 4

1. Title	63	Definition of probability
2. Introductory Material	64	History of probability
3. Prerequisite Material	ix	Chapter 1

Previewing Chapter 5

1. Title	95	Definition of binomial
2. Introductory Material	96	Importance of binomial distributions
3. Section 5.3	107	Repeated trials
4. Prerequisite Material	ix	Chapters 1, 2, 3, 4

Previewing Chapter 6

1. Title	119	Definition of normal
2. Introductory Material	120	Importance of normal distribution
3. Table 5	349	Area under the normal curve
4. Z Scores	129	Other methods of scoring
5. Area Under the Curve	137	Relationship of geometry and probability

Important Features	Page	Concept to Be Introduced
6. Section 6.5	151	Relationship between normal & binomial distributions
7. Prerequisite Material	ix	Chapters 1, 2, 3, 4, 5

Previewing Chapter 7

1. Title	197	Definition of hypothesis
2. Introductory Material	198	Relationship of probability and hypothesis testing
3. Section 8.2	207	Last section covered in chapter 8
4. Prerequisite Material	ix	Chapters 1, 2, 3, 4, 6

Previewing Chapter 8

1. Title	249	Definition of correlation
2. Introductory Material	250	Importance of correlation
3. Scattergram	251	Other types of graphing
4. Section 9.3	269	The other section to be covered
5. Linear Correlation	274	Another statistic
6. Prerequisite Material	ix	Chapter 1

Previewing Chapter 9

1. Title	292	Definition of independence
2. Chi Square Distribution	298	Method of determining independence
3. Prerequisite Material	ix	Chapters 1, 2, 3, 4, 5

II.   ORAL

A.   Focus and Ongoing Questions

Focus Questions for Sections 2.1 & 2.2

1.   Define what is meant by the word "population."

2.   Describe the relationship between the sample and the population in a study.

3.   Explain the factors which make a sample random.

4.   Describe a random number table and illustrate its usefulness.

5.   State the factors which determine how well the characteristics of the sample can be expected to reflect the characteristics of the population from which the sample was drawn.

6.   Describe the method you would use to generate a random sample of students from this class.

7.   Define what is meant by descriptive statistics.

8.   Compare the advantages of organizing data into tables, bar graphs, pictograms, and circle graphs.

9.   Organize the data below into a table, a bar graph, a pictogram, and a circle graph. Be creative!

   Bob, Carol, and Ted are collecting soda cans for recycling. Bob collects 4 cans on Monday, 3 on Tuesday, 5 on Wednesday, 9 on Thursday, and 1 on Friday. Carol collects 2 on Monday, 3 on Tuesday, 8 on Wednesday, 1 on Thursday, and 7 on Friday. Ted collects 3 on Monday, 3 on Tuesday, 2 on Wednesday, 4 on Thursday, and 3 on Friday.

Ongoing Questions for Sections 2.1 & 2.2

1.   After the distribution of the following questionnaire:

   a.   How often do you brush your teeth?
   b.   How many dates have you had this past year?
   c.   Are you wearing the same underwear you had on yesterday?

   I ask, How accurately do you expect the data obtained to reflect reality? Why?

   What can we say, in general, about responses to personal questions?

2. During World War II the National Opinion Research Center sent out two different sets of interviewers (Set A and Set B) to survey 500 blacks in a southern city. Here are their results:

Question 1: Would Negroes be treated better or worse if the Japanese conquered the USA?

	Better	Worse	No Opinion
Set A	2%	45%	53%
Set B	9%	25%	66%

Question 2: Do you think that it is more important to concentrate on beating the Axis or making democracy work better at home?

	Beating the Axis
Set A	62%
Set B	39%

Hypothesize why these two sets of interviewers might have gotten such different results? Which set of interviewers were black? What can you say, in general, about the factor of trust/suspicion between the subject and questioner?

3. Latadope Pharmaceutical Company has a new product for the common cold. They claim 98% of sufferers who use the product got relief within a few days.

Are you impressed by this claim? Why (not)?

"Proper treatment will cure a cold in 7 days, but left to itself a cold will hang on for a week!"

4. My psychoanalyst told me recently that based on her observances of people, most people are neurotic!

Do you value this "authority's opinion"? Might her "sample" have biased her conclusion?

5. An interviewer must stop Oriental men on the street to question them. The men must be over 40 years of age. Two men, who appear to be in that category approach. One is neatly dressed and carries an attache case. The other is in dirty work clothes and looks surly. Finish the story.

6. Claim: 4 out of 5 dentists recommend Trident for their patients who chew gum.

What is deceptive about this claim?

7. During the Spanish-American War the death rate in the Navy was 9 in 1,000 while the death rate in New York City was 16 in 1,000. On that basis the Navy claimed it was safer to be in the Navy than in New York City! Was the claim "true"? Why (not)?

Focus & Ongoing Questions

Meeting #4 (section 2.3)

1. How is a histogram different from a bar graph?

2. How does one construct a histogram from a frequency polygon?

3. What is the relationship between class limits and class boundaries?

4. What is the difference between rounding-up and rounding-off?

1. Work problem 6 on page 33 in class.

Meeting #5 (section 3.1)

1. What was the Roman havaria?

2. Explain why a union leader and a boss might use different averages in labor contract negotiations?

3. Construct a distribution in which the mean is large than the median.

4. Why is the mean greatly affected by extreme scores?

1. Work problem 2 on page 46 in class.

Meeting #6 (section 3.2)

1. What is the difference between the "typical" score and the "spread" of the scores?

2. How are squaring and square rooting related?

3. As s gets smaller, the scores in the distribution get . . .

4. Why did the author change approximation symbols on page 51?

1. Work problem 1 on page 55 in class.

Meeting #7 (section 3.3)

1. What is a frequency table?

2. What is the advantage of grouping data?

3. Is the formula on page 55 for s familiar? Why?

4. Does the formula for the mean of grouped data give
    the same number as the standard formula for
    ungrouped data?

1. Work problem 4 on page 58 in class.

Meeting #8 (section 3.3 again)

1. Is it possible for the range and standard deviation
    to be equal? Give an example.

2. Construct a distribution where the mode equals the
    mean.

3. What statistics typify a distribution?

4. What statistic measures the spread of a
    distribution?

1. Work problem 6 on page 60 in class.

Meeting #9 (section 4.1)

1. What is the probability that today is Sunday?

2. What is the probability that this is a stat class?

3. What are the three ways of determining the
    probability of an event

4. There is a 30% chance of rain tomorrow. What does
    that mean?

1. Work problem 6 on page 70 in class.

Meeting #10 (section 4.2)

1. What do these mean:

    I am a Catholic and an American.
    I am a Catholic or an American.

2. Give examples of independent events.

3. Give examples of dependent events

4. Give examples of mutually exclusive events.

1. Work problem 8 on page 80 in class.

Meeting #11 (section 4.3)

1. What is the area under any histogram of a probability distribution?

2. Compare a parameter and a statistic.

3. What is a random variable?

4. What is a discrete variable?

1. Work problem 4 on page 89 in class.

Meeting #12 (section 4.3 again)

1. What is probability?

2. What is the difference between continuous and discrete random variables?

3. How can relative frequency be used to estimate probability?

4. What is the sample space for an experiment?

1. Work problem 1 on page 90 in class.

Meeting #13 (section 9.1)

1. Give an example of two things which are positively correlated.

2. Give an example of two things which are negatively correlated.

3. Give an example of two things which are uncorrelated.

4. How does the shape of the scattergram indicate linear correlation?

1. Do problem 8 on page 256 in class.

Meeting #14 (section 9.3)

1. What is the difference between the sum of the squares and the square of the sum?

2. Show a scattergram indicating a 0 correlation.

3. Show a scattergram indicating a strong positive correlation.

4. Show a scattergram indicating a strong negative correlation.

1. Work problem 6 on page 280 in class.

Meeting #15 (section 9.3 again)

1. Why do you need paired data to compute the correlation coefficient?

2. What does r = -1 indicate?

3. What does r = 0 indicate?

4. How can one compute $\sqrt{564}$ using the table in the text?

1. Work problem 1 a, c on page 287 in class.

Meeting # 16 (section 5.1)

1. What does the prefix "bi-" mean?

2. What is the relationship of p and q?

3. If you flip a fair coin 100 times, what is the probability of getting 50 heads? Is it 50%?

4. Give an example of a trinomial experiment.

1. Work problem 4 on page 100 in class.

Meeting #17 (section 5.2)

1. What is the probability of getting 3 heads in 4 flips of a fair coin?

2. What does n! mean?

3. Use the table in the text to find $C_{5,2}$ and verify by formula.

4. What do "at least" and "at most" mean?

1. Work problem 8 on page 107 in class.

Meeting #18 (section 5.3)

1. What is the area under the graph of a binomial distribution on page 108?

2. Use the table in the book to discover properties of Pascal's triangle.

3. Is the graph of a binomial distribution symmetric?

4. What does np equal for a binomial distribution?

1. Work problem 4 on page 114 in class.

Note: Focus and Ongoing Questions were prepared for all class meetings. However, only those Focus and Ongoing Questions for lessons 1 through 18 are included here because of space considerations.

A Learning Guide Sampler

Prepared by Jeffrey Davis, Ingrid De Cicco, Mary Beth Early, Nicholas Gilroy, George Groman, and Olga Vega; LaGuardia Community College, City University of New York.

The following selection of learning guides produced by faculty in several disciplines should demonstrate the range of possibilities for developing curricular materials based upon the principles laid out in this book. Materials are keyed to specific strategies so that you can check back easily.

STRATEGY 1:   GAUGING WRITING SKILLS

A.   Course: Introduction to Literature

Most families have a set of stories about family events and
(or) family members, stories told again and again. In the
space provided write about two paragraphs in which you tell
one of your family stories.

B.   Course: Phonetics I

All human beings must communicate to live. Sometimes our
communications succeed and sometimes they don't. Please
write a few paragraphs (up to a page or two) in which you
tell about one of your experiences as a communicator. Write
about either a very good experience or a very bad experience.

STRATEGY 2:   GAUGING ORAL COMMUNICATION SKILLS

A.   Course: Occupational Therapy Media & Application I

Directions: You will be given a large sheet of white paper
(12 x 18 inches) and a few magic markers. Use this paper to
draw a map of your life, starting from the moment of your
birth. Your map should show the people or events which led
to your choice of occupational therapy as a career and
LaGuardia as the college to prepare you for this career. You
have 10 minutes to complete you map. Then each student will
present and explain, in no more than five minutes, his or her
map to the class.

B.   Course: Business Management

In this course we will be dealing with approaches to money
acquisition and management. Take five minutes to think about
your first scheme, as a child, for making money. Then tell
the class about this scheme in a minute or two.

STRATEGY 3:   GAUGING LISTENING SKILLS

A.   Course: Word Processing I

As you know, both communication skills and technical skills
are critical for the secretary. Today we'll measure your
ability to listen carefully. The videotape I will play now
offers an introduction to the machine transcriber that we
will be using over the next few weeks. Listen carefully,

take notes if you like, and then I will distribute a list of
fifteen questions designed as a check on how well you listen.
THIS WILL NOT BE GRADED AS A TEST; it is designed only to
show us how much we have to concentrate on listening skills
this quarter.

B.   American History

Today I will lecture on the major differences between the
"old" and the "new" history. I am distributing an outline of
this lecture before I begin. Notice that some of the main
points (Roman numeral headings) and the supporting points
(alphabetical headings) are filled in while others are left
blank. Listen carefully to the lecture, and fill in the
missing points.

STRATEGY 4:   GAUGING READING SKILLS (CLOZE TEST)

A.   Course: Phonetics I (Passage taken from Articulation and
     Voice by Robert King and Eleanor D. Michael, New York:
     Macmillan, 1978, p. 182.)

     In the double-spaced passage below, please fill in each blank
     with what you think is the appropriate word. The passage
     comes from a text we will be using. This activity will help
     me guide you through the course reading. YOUR ANSWERS WILL
     NOT BE GRADED. (Two extra single-spaced paragraphs have been
     provided, an introduction and a conclusion, to help give you
     a better idea of the subject matter.)

Duration of Vowels

The duration of a vowel, of course, is how long you hold it. A vowel is a sound that can be sustained or prolonged. How long you prolong a vowel depends on three factors: (1) the nature of the vowel itself (some vowels are inherently longer--in English, at least--than other vowels); (2) whether the vowel occurs in a stressed syllable (and, if so, the degree of stress); and (3) the vowel's position in a syllable and its neighboring sounds.

We said that some 1_____ are naturally longer (in

2_____) than other vowels. Some 3_____ dispute that

statement, because 4_____ you could hold on 5_____ any

vowel for a 6_____ time. But, in connected 7_____,

some vowels are given 8_____ duration than others. True,

9_____ are other factors involved 10_____, but /u/

(oo)is 11_____ held longer than /U/ (12_____). Poets

know the value of using long and short 13_____ (We are not

talking 14_____ diacritics in the dictionaries, 15_____

about the length of 16_____ a vowel lasts.) to 17_____

their purposes in poems. Edgar Allan Poe wrote 18_____

essay about the use of 19_____ and the choice of

20_____ to create certain moods. 21_____ must give

vowels their 22_____ length to catch the 23_____ and

rhythm built into 24_____ speech patterns.

Another factor 25_____ the length of time 26_____ vowel

gets is syllabic 27_____. We make some syllables

28_____ out by giving them 29_____ stress (prominence)

than other 30_____. We accomplish this stressing

31_____ the syllable by increasing 32_____, raising

pitch, and increasing 33_____ duration of the vowel.

34_____ stretch out syllables we 35_____ to stand out.

Stressed 36_____ are longer, because the 37_____ are

held longer. You 38_____ check this out for 39_____.

Say the words "no" 40_____ "piano" out loud. Is

41_____ "o" in each of 42_____ length? No, because in

43_____ first word the syllable 44_____ stressed and in

the 45_____ is unstressed.

Finally, how long a vowel will be sustained depends also on what
position it has in a syllable and in a word and on what sound
follows. Try the words "row" and "romance" out loud. The /o/
phoneme of the first word is longer than the /o/ of the second
word. This is partly so because the first is in a stressed
syllable and the second in an unstressed syllable.

B.   Course: Freshman Advisory Seminar (Seminar offered by
     Department of Student Services, and passage is taken from the
     LaGuardia Handbook, LaGuardia Community College, the City
     University of New York, 1981-82, p. 6.)

     The Career Resource Center (CRC) houses special resources to
     answer your questions about transfer and careers.

The (1)_____ has a library of senior (2)_____

catalogs (over 800 to (3)_____) from general guides to

(4)_____ four-year colleges and (5)_____

fields of (6)_____ and individual colleges

(7)_____ with (8)_____ contracts, admission

requirements, financial (9)_____ data, and other

(10)_____ to help (11)_____ get to know other

(12)_____. Use of the combined resources of a

(13)_____, the Career Resource (14)_____ and

the Admissions/Transfer (15)_____ will help you with

(16)_____ about continuing your (17)_____.

Also available in the CRC (18)_____ a wide range of

(19)_____ exploration aids; pamphlets

(20)_____ publications on (21)_____ of

occupations (22)_____ on present (23)_____

employment opportunities in different (24)_____, and

people and (25)_____ to contact for more

(26)_____.

A unique (27)_____ available is a computerized guidance

information (28)_____ that provides access to

information on (29)_____ and college programs. By

(30)_____, students may arrange (31)_____

computer time to (32)_____ information on their

specific (33)_____ of college choice, or

(34)_____ may use the system to (35)_____ for

a career or (36)_____ program appropriate to their

(37)_____. A CRC (38)_____ member will be

(39)_____ to show (40)_____ around and

familiarize you with the (41)_____ facilities.

STRATEGY 5: DEVELOPING BRIEF WRITING TASKS

A. Course: Principles of Finance

   A commercial bank can be described as a supermarket of
   financial services where consumers can select a number of
   offerings that suit their needs.
        Imagine that you are a bank officer in charge of public
   relations. Prepare a one-page flyer in which you identify
   (point out) four services available at your bank and you
   explain (make understandable) what is special about these
   services. Pay particular attention to your introductory
   paragraph, which should engage the reader's attention
   immediately.

B. Course: Occupational Therapy

Directions: Answer the following question. Your answer
should be about two or three pages long, double-spaced and
typewritten. Essays must be in complete sentences, must use
paragraphs, and must be submitted on time to receive full
credit.

Question: Purtilo, in Chapter 10 of Health Professional/
Patient Interaction, shows how the cultural and personal
biases of health providers can influence relationships
with patients. Reflect on your own cultural and personal
background and biases. Of the following three individuals,
which one would you find most easy to understand and respond
to in a helping relationship?

--An upper-middle-class corporation president, hospitalized
  for a malignant brain tumor. This person is a "self-made
  man" who fought his way up from poverty. He has told the
  nurse that he thinks poor people are poor because they are
  "stupid and lazy."

--An elderly widow, suffering from diabetes and poor
  circulation, and now living in a nursing home. She was
  born in Eastern Europe and speaks little English. She is
  very irritable and believes that young people nowadays are
  only interested in themselves (and in drugs, money, and
  sex) and are "the children of the devil."

--A very attractive 26-year-old man, who is an ex-convict and
  a drug addict. He is in the hospital for detoxification
  and evaluation. He believes it is a "waste of time to try
  to make it in society."

Explain your answer in terms of your own background and
biases. (To explain means "to give reasons for.")

Hints:

1. In the first paragraph of your essay, be sure to mention
    the individual you selected. In this paragraph you
    should also state the main point you wish to make about
    your own cultural background and biases. The rest of the
    essay should give specific details that support the
    points you made in your first paragraph. The last
    paragraph should be a brief summary of your main points.

2. Write an outline of your paper before you begin to write.

3. Check you final copy for writing errors.

STRATEGY 6:   OVERSEEING THE WRITING PROCESS

Course: Freshman Advisory Seminar (Seminar offered by the
Department of Student Services)

(A counselor produced the following materials in response to the
assignment she would soon give to the class. Copies of these
materials along with the assignment appear in her learning
guide.)

Assignment: In the last session you obtained information from
the Career Resource Center on your chosen career. For this
activity write a page explaining how this career matches your
personal characteristics (skills, interests, and abilities).

Sample of Teacher's Prewriting

Career - Counseling

~~Why~~ How did I choose this field?

Education —
   1. Interested in political science
      Specifically — Latin American
         history
      Read books on politics, econ.
         analysis of social conditions
            history
   2. Seminars and classes on
      racism, psychology, social
      science, Puerto Rican history, culture.
   3. Exchange student - studied
      in P. Rico for a summer.
   4. Courses on politics in N.Y.C.
      Black history courses
      Courses at Yale Univ. — Politics
         in N.Y.C.
   5. Internships — Community agencies
      Worked in high school
         (alternative)
      ~~Old age~~ geriatrics — senior
         citizens
      Family day care — counselor

Self - (Values)
  Change the system - advocacy
    work.
  Helps people.
  Enjoy contact with people.
  Difference working with people
    in theory and reality.
  Manipulate system to assist
    and get the services they need.

Why I chose this field —
  Continuing provide direct services.
  Science — techniques — methods,
    theory.
  Effective - feel doing it correctly.
  Didn't care about money.
  Work with other people who
    share my goals.
  Change agent.
  People would change through
    intervention.
  Field matches with my personal
    characteristics — concerned,
    friendly, talkative, creative.

Sample of Teacher's Rough Draft

My interest in counseling stemmed from a personal desire and concern for working with people ~~as an agent~~ in this type of setting ~~for social change~~. As a counselor I could work within an organization or school and serve as an advocate in counseling. Counselors ~~work with four agencies~~ are trained professionals who work in various organizations.

Some are community based organizations such as schools, hospitals, and many mental health clinics, social service agencies such as foster care, adoptive services, day care, etc. other types of organizations that provide direct service to people who need help.

I have been and continue to be interested in not only providing direct services but also functioning in an advocacy to people

An advocate is an individual
role so that these institutions who

responds to and meets the needs of

their clients. Client is a term used to

describe the individuals who are the

recipients of the services of an agency.

As an advocate I would function as an

An agent for
agent for social change. This interest
social change is an individual who is dedicated
and commitment developed early in my
and skillful in bringing about change.
undergraduate education. I was interested

in political science and took courses in

that discipline. I also took courses in

sociology, psychology, and Latin American

history. As I began to analyze the

economic and social conditions affecting

minorities in this country, I decided

to choose a career in which I could

work ~~faithfully~~ with clients in helping

them deal with their problems.

In addition to having a theoretical

understanding of their problems, as an

individual I am warm and friendly

and I enjoy being involved with

other people. In essence, I am a

people-oriented person. This combination

of ~~skills~~ knowledge, my values, and

interest was the basis for my decision

to identify a career that would

complement who I am as a person.

Another
~~One~~ major factor contributing to my

decision was that I am also a minority,

who has background and economic status was similar to that one of minorities today. I believed then that to be an effective helper, & that that the helper had to be someone who would had an identical background as the clients. So that only Through a combination of experience, skills, and theory could I become an effective professional.

Skills effort — committed to working to ameliorate the social conditions which adversely affect the population.

Sample of Teacher's Final Copy

Counselors are trained professionals who work in various organizations providing a variety of services. Some of these organizations are community-based agencies such as mental health clinics, day-care centers, foster and adoption agencies, hospitals, schools, etc. My interest in counseling stemmed from a personal concern for people in these types of settings and a desire to work with them.

I think I have always been interested in providing direct services to people and also in serving as an advocate for them. The advocacy role is vital: An institution that you work for must meet the needs of the clients it is servicing or else cease to be of service. I have always been interested in seeing that people get what they need to lead fulfilled lives, that systems work for human ends.

This interest and commitment developed early in my undergraduate education. I took courses in political science, psychology, sociology, and Latin American history. As I began to analyze the economic and social conditions affecting minorities in this country, I decided to choose a career in which I could work directly with minorities, helping them deal with their problems. In addition to having a theoretical understanding of their problems, as an individual I am a warm, friendly, open person who enjoys involvement. The combination of knowledge, values, and interest was the basis for my decision to choose a career that would draw on who I am as a person.

Another major factor was my social background. As a poor minority whose background was similar to those of minorities receiving services, I considered myself able to be a more effective helper than someone coming from a different background. Through an integration of personal experiences and the skills acquired as a trained counselor, I became an effective professional, able to find deep satisfaction in helping others find the same.

Teacher's Plan for Overseeing Drafts

Students will make 5 copies of their drafts. They will bring
their copies to class and form a cluster. Each student will read
the other students' papers and will make suggestions. I will be
moving from group to group and will provide feedback to the
groups.

A feedback list that includes the following will be
distributed:

1. Does the student introduce his/her topic in the first

    sentence?

    _____

    _____

2. Do the ideas follow one another? Point out strong spots

    as well as weak ones.

    _____

    _____

3. Is there sufficient detail?

    _____

4. Are the ideas expressed in complete and sentences?

    Where would you like to see some changes?

    _____

    _____

5. Are there places where ideas could be communicated more

    effectively?

    _____

    _____

6. Note any spelling errors. What kinds of errors should

    the writer concentrate on?

    _____

    _____

STRATEGY 7:   CREATING RESEARCH ASSIGNMENTS

Course: Principles of Finance

I. Write a research report analyzing one of today's major
economic problems and the President's responses to this
problem. (To analyze means "to examine the parts of
something.") In the report you should:

A. Identify the economic issue (inflation, unemployment,
and so on) which you think is most troubling the
nation. Explain your choice.

B. Identify the solutions, if any, that the President has
proposed and/or begun implementing. (Be sure to
explain the Administration's plan in as much detail as
possible.)

C. Evaluate (that is, give your own judgments about) the
Administration's economic plan. Be sure to identify
those parts of the plan you favor and those you believe
are poor.

II. Collection: The report is due March 15. However, I will
collect parts of your work according to the following
schedule:

A. Note cards on at least two readings: January 15

B. Outline: February 5

C. Rough draft of introductory paragraph (including thesis
statement): February 18

D. Rough draft of complete report (optional):   March 1

I will return all these drafts with comments.

III. Manuscript Preparation

A. Research. The major portion of your research should be
acquired from periodicals and newspapers. Use at least
five sources. Take notes on note cards, as indicated
in the learning guide.

The Reader's Guide to Periodical Literature is an
excellent source to locate magazine articles.

The New York Times Index will guide you to appropriate
articles from the New York Times. Do not hesitate to
ask library personnel to show you how to use these
helpful indexes.

B. Prepare an outline of your report before beginning to
write. The outline should have three major parts, as

indicated in the assignment. Outlines can be very helpful in organizing your ideas and staying on the topic.

C. The report must include a <u>bibliography</u> identifying the research sources used. (See the handout included in your learning guide for correct bibliography format.)

D. The report should be typewritten and double-spaced. It should be about five pages long.

E. Check your report carefully before typing to catch any writing errors which may be in the report.

<u>Good luck</u>, and get started soon.

STRATEGY 8: ASSIGNING FIELD AND LABORATORY REPORTS

Course: Critical Issues in Health

<u>REPORT ON A VISIT TO A</u>
<u>HEALTH-RELATED FACILITY</u>

<u>Assignment</u>: This assignment requires you to visit a health-related facility, to record your observations, and to write a report.

The objectives of this assignment are:

1. to increase awareness of health resources in the community

2. to observe the operation of a specific facility

3. to differentiate between observation and evaluation when collecting data during a scheduled visit

4. to write a description and an evaluation of this health program

<u>Procedures</u>: Choose a place that you would like to visit, for example: Planned Parenthood, a drug rehabilitation center (Phoenix House), a mental health center, an abortion center, an obstetrics division of a hospital, a nursing home, the Health Department Nutrition Program or VD Prevention Unit, and so on. Call or write to request an interview and a tour of the facility. It is important to be sure that an authorized person can spend some time showing you around and answering your questions.
Study the travel directions and know your expected arrival time and the person to report to. If in doubt as to an estimated travel time from your home, contact the Transit Authority for information. Allow additional time to arrive prior to the scheduled time.

Consider the setting you are to visit when deciding how to dress for the day.

Take this report handout with you as a guide sheet. Also take a pen or pencil and record information directly on the handout. You will write a report (see assignment below) based on your notes.

Due Dates:

      1. Statement of appointment to include:

         Name of agency/facility _____

         Date and time of appointment _____

         Authorized person with whom
         the appointment was made _____
                     Due: February 1

      2. Completed report form (which consists
         of the description and evaluation)
              Due: February 15

      3. Agency report, first draft
              Due: March 3

      4. Agency report, final draft
              Due: March 10

Note to student: Before items 2, 3, and 4 under "due dates" are handed in, be sure to check your work carefully and seek help if needed. Read, complete, and sign the appropriate section of the proofreading and correction tear-off. Detach and staple it to the assignment being handed in. The following worksheet will help you prepare for the visit and organize you information for the written report.

Name _____ Student # _____

HLT course and section _____

Date of visit _____ Time of appointment _____

Program visited _____

Address _____

Name and title of staff member _____

I. Description

Your first effort is to observe and to record what you see.
Description requires that you rely upon sensory resources
to identify the physical elements of the agency and its
people. (You will have to ask questions of your tour
leader in order to supplement your own observations.)

A. What did the place look like? Was it spacious, bright?
    How many different kinds of rooms were there?

B. What kinds of employees were available? Which of their
    tasks did you observe?

C. What population does the agency serve? Tell their age,
    where they come from, some of their problems, and some
    of the programs in which they participate.

D. Who funds the program and to whom do the program
    administrators report?

E. What kinds of equipment or specialized materials or
    techniques did you see? For what purposes are they
    used?

F. What kind of relevant printed materials did you notice?
    What information did you learn from them?

II. Evaluation

Now you must make some judgments about this agency. An
evaluation requires that you use your observations to form
an opinion.

A. What were your impressions of the facility?

B. What were your feelings as you saw the clients? How
did the population served differ from what you had
expected?

C. What were your reactions to the health careers you
observed? Did you consider the number of staff to be
adequate?

D. In your estimation, did the facility appear to be well
organized? What changes would you suggest?

E. What impressed you most about your visit? What did you
like best? What made you feel uncomfortable?

III. Written Report

On separate paper, write an essay of about two pages in
which you explain the program for a person who is
considering using its services but who has little knowledge
about it. Use the responses you wrote directly on this
handout as the basis for your report. In your introduction
(a paragraph or two), name the agency and describe its most
important physical features. Name the various funding

sources, the sponsoring organization, and whether the program is voluntary, government, nonprofit, or proprietary.

In your next paragraphs, identify the makeup of the clients/patients served by the program. (consider areas such as age, sex, and diagnoses.) List the variety of health professionals and the program uses. Then (in a few paragraphs) evaluate the agency and make a recommendation to your reader as to whether or not the person should use its services.

Final drafts must be typed and must follow guidelines for manuscript preparation.

STRATEGY 9: STRUCTURING QUESTIONS TO FOSTER PURPOSEFUL LISTENING AND DISCUSSION

Course: Introduction to Poetry

Focus Questions: In order to focus our session today, I have listed questions on the board to guide our discussion of "The Road Not Taken." At appropriate points we will attempt to pull together what we've said in order to answer the questions.

1. Who is the speaker in the poem, and what do you know about him?

2. What is the occasion of the poem?

3. What "point" does the poem make about choices in life?

4. How does the language of the poem contribute to its meaning?

STRATEGY 10: DEVELOPING ORAL ASSIGNMENTS

A. Course: Principles of Finance

Almost every week, some important economic or financial event makes the newspaper headlines. The event may be about the merger of two troubled savings banks, or it might concern something about the President's budget, or it may deal with the difficulties facing the Federal Reserve Bank.

For each week of the term three students will be assigned to report to our class about a financial event that happened during the past week. When your assigned date to report comes, you should have prepared an outline detailing your three-minute report on the chosen event. Be sure to explain:

a. What has happened?

b. Who is involved?

c. Who is affected by the event?

d. Why it is of broad general interest?

The use of an outline or notes is permitted. Reading a prepared report word for word is not permitted.

B. Course: Freshman Advisory Seminar (Seminar offered by the Department of Student Services)

The purpose of this assignment is to help you learn and develop skills in oral communication. Oral communication is the ability to speak effectively to another person or to a group of people. Speaking is an important skill in our everyday life. We are constantly transmitting our ideas, opinions, and feelings orally. Speaking is an essential skill needed in school, at home, and in your future careers. In essence, it is the skill we rely on most often in communicating with other people.

Assignment: Students experience many different types of problems. Some are of a personal nature, others are educational. One of the goals of this seminar is to help you learn how to solve problems. For this assignment each of you will be given a specific problem. You are to solve this problem using the points on the "Steps in Problem Solving" sheet and then to prepare a five-minute presentation. In your presentation, begin by paraphrasing the problem that was assigned to you. Paraphrase means "to restate in your own words." Then describe the technique used to solve the problem. Be sure to practice your presentation, using a tape recorder or a friend or relative as a listener. Be aware of your time. Ask yourself whether your words are clear. Have you communicated to the group how you've solved the problem? Consider the points that the class and I will consider as we listen (see Evaluation below).

Sample Problems:

Maria is a freshman and is in an ESL 096 class. She understands a little bit of English but does not know how to write. She is having difficulties understanding the teacher, who she thinks talks too fast. She feels the assignments of the class are not possible for her to complete since her writing skills are limited. She thinks the teacher's expectations are too high. What can she do?

Helen is a sophomore who has completed 45 credits. She is majoring in data processing and has a grade point average of 1.02. She has been notified that she is on probation. Helen feels that she has had problems with two of her data processing instructors and that is why she is being placed on probation. What should she do?

Evaluation: I will evaluate you on:
--how well you paraphrase the problem.
--the thoroughness with which you apply the steps to solve the problem.
--the organization of your presentation.
--clarity of voice, tone, pitch.

Steps in Problem Solving

Step 1. Exploration

The first step is to explore what is the concern or problem. To do this, describe in detail all the facts or information by listing them. Do not worry whether they are applicable or not. You will select the most important ones in the next step.

Step 2. Identify the Problem

After you have described in detail the problem, you can analyze it. To analyze means "to examine all the elements and the relationships of these elements to one another." In other words, you will examine all the factors listed in the previous step and how they relate to one another. Once you have studied all the factors, make a summary of the problem by stating it in the form of a goal. You may want to know how widespread the problem is or how it began.

Step 3. Determine the Individual or Groups Interested in Working on the Problem

Here you explore whether the individuals or members are interested in working out the problem.

Step 4. Information-Gathering About the Problem

Here you collect data, facts, or important information about the problem.

Step 5. Planning for the Evaluation of the Problem

You have briefly identified your goals in Step 2. Decide on activities or strategies to achieve this goal. This means you develop a plan. Here's where you decide what you are going to do.

Step 6. Implementation of the Plan

You are now ready to carry out or engage in the activities you planned. Here you identify who is going to do what. How much time is it going to take?

Step 7.   Evaluation

Now you will assess how effective your plan and
activities were. Did your plan solve the problem?
Did it need to be changed? As you implemented this
plan, did other problems arise?

Step 8.   Forecasting the Future

Where do you go from here? Must you set up new
goals? If you must, then you begin with the
exploration process.

STRATEGY 11:   PROVIDING HELPFUL REACTIONS TO STUDENTS' ORAL
RESPONSES

Course: Critical Issues in Health

The ability to present ideas and feelings orally and the ability
to ask and respond to questions appropriately are skills needed
for success in most health-related careers. One of our goals
this semester will be to help one another grow in competency in
oral skills. We are going to pay careful attention to what we
say and how we say it. In particular, we will focus on:

How we say

1.   Appropriateness of Answers. A question may ask for a fact,
      an opinion, an interpretation, or an evaluation. If you are
      asked, "Which type of drug is used as an appetite
      depressant?" and you answer, "I don't think diet pills are
      any good," you have given an opinion and not the fact that
      was called for.

How we say it

2.   Volume. Are you speaking loud enough to be heard and
      understood?

3.   Verbal Fillers. Is your speech clear of "um," "you know,"
      and all those other interjections we make to fill the
      silences between the thoughts we express?

4.   Pronunciation. Are you pronouncing words clearly and
      correctly?

We will attend to these areas by repeating the behavior
(mirroring) or by identifying the kind of behavior (labeling).
In mirroring for verbal fillers, for example, if someone said
"um," someone else in the class repeats "um," calling attention
to the speaker's use of fillers. Labeling, in contrast, involves
identifying the kind of problem: for example, if a student gives

an opinion instead of a fact (see 1 above), someone in the class
would say "opinion," to call attention to the response.

STRATEGY 12:   PREVIEWING READINGS

Course: Occupational Therapy

Text Preview of Health Professional/Patient Interaction, by
Purtilo

This is an oral classroom activity in which the instructor will
go over the following questions with the class. This activity
will acquaint you with the major features of your text.

1. Note the title of the book. What does it mean?
    How is it relevant to occupational therapy?

2. Turn to page xiii, which is marked CONTENTS. Observe the
    following features:

    a. The book is divided into PARTS, which are listed in
        boldfaced type. Each PART contains several CHAPTERS.

    b. Each CHAPTER is outlined, and pages are listed for each
        topic in the CHAPTER.

    Use the table of contents to locate where in your book you
would find information on working with patients with terminal
illnesses.

3. Turn to page 281, which is marked INDEX.
    What is the purpose of an index?
    Use the index to locate where in your book you could read
    about elderly patients.

    Elderly patients is not listed in the index. What other
    words might mean the same?

    _____

    _____

    _____

    Look up these phrases in the index.

Section Preview

1. Turn to page 95, which is a summary for PART III.

    a. What is the title of PART III? What does the title
        (Determinants of Effective Interaction between Health
        Professional and Patient) mean?

    b. There are three chapters in PART III; each is outlined on page 95. Verbal Communication (Chapter 8) and Nonverbal Communication (Chapter 9) are obviously related to interaction. What does the title of Chapter 10 (Cultural and Personal Biases as Determinants of Effectiveness) mean? How is this related to effective interaction?

2. Turn to page 97. Observe the following:

   a. A boldfaced heading (Constructs of Language) indicates a major topic. On page 98 another major topic is introduced. What is it?

   b. On page 99, smaller boldfaced type indicates a subtopic, a part of the major topic. What is the subtopic?

   c. On page 100, there is a passage set off by horizontal lines and smaller type. This passage has a small number at the end of it. Why is this?

3. Turn to page 128. At the bottom of the page a list of references begins. These are for all of PART III (Chapters 8, 9, 10). Find the reference which matches the passage quoted on page 100.

   How else could you use the list of references?

Summary: This preview should be of value to you in reading your text. We have covered the main features. Is there anything else you would like to know about this book?

STRATEGIES 13 and 14: PREPARING READING GUIDES AND INTRODUCING DIFFICULT VOCABULARY

Course: Introduction to Literature

   D. H. Lawrence's "The Rocking-Horse Winner" (pages 325-337)

D. H. Lawrence's "The Rocking-Horse Winner" (included in Perrine's Story and Structure, pages 325-337) is a tale of love and hate as it exists between a mother and her children. The story also focuses on the meaning of luck and the connections between luck and money. If you think about these definitions and connections, you should have a clear sense of what Lawrence is attempting in his story.

   In reading the story, you will find it helpful to do the following things:

   I. Define (give the meaning of) love as it appears to exist between the mother and her children.

   II. Compare and contrast (show similarities and differences) between the definition of love presented in the story and your own view. It is worth noting here that the dictionary will <u>not</u> be of help.

III. <u>Define</u> (give the meaning of) <u>luck</u> as it is perceived by the mother and as it is perceived by Paul, her son.

IV. <u>Compare and contrast</u> (show similarities and differences between) the definition of <u>luck</u> in the story and your own view. Here again, the dictionary will <u>not</u> be of help.

V. Why does the mother describe the father as <u>unlucky</u>? Why is it (according to the mother) better to be <u>born lucky</u> than to be <u>born rich</u>?

VI. Is the father <u>unlucky</u>? If so, why?

VII. Lawrence tells us that the very walls in this middle-class home seem to whisper, "There must be more money, there must be more money."

A. <u>Describe</u> (give details of) what Paul's mother will do with money if she gets it.

B. <u>Describe</u> (give details of) Paul's plan for using the money he has won.

C. <u>Evaluate</u> (give reasons for agreeing or disagreeing with) the plans of Paul and his mother, described above.

VIII. <u>Explain</u> (account for) the role of the rocking horse in Lawrence's story.

IX. Is the story you have read a <u>fantasy</u>, or can the events described really take place? Why do you think so?

X. Below are listed some words you may (or may not) know. Read them carefully, look up those you don't know in the dictionary, and then answer the following questions:

A. Which terms are British rather than American?

B. Why is it important to know the meanings of the British terms?

C. Which of the words listed help us understand the characters (people) in the story?

D. Does the language used suggest anything about Lawrence's <u>point of view</u> or <u>style as a writer</u>? Explain.

assertion	parry	remonstrate
bonny	shilling	prance
stealth	pound	uncanny
frenzy	lucre	surging
careered	governess	trivet
batman	emancipated	ecstasy

Note: It will probably be helpful to write the definitions of
        words you don't know in the margins of the pages where
        they are located. It may also be helpful to write words
        on 3" x 5" cards with the definitions on the back of each
        card. In this way, you will have a means of rapid review.

STRATEGY 15:   A HOLISTIC APPROACH TO CONTENT: INTEGRATED SKILLS
REINFORCEMENT (ISR)

Sample of General Statements on Course Requirements prepared for
two Learning Guides, one for a course in Occupational Therapy and
one for a Freshman Advisory Seminar offered by the Department of
Student Services.

Course: Occupational Therapy Media and Application I

I. Writing Activities

    A. Assignments: As a student in SCO 210, you must
        complete the following writing tasks:

        1. A paragraph about your preferred learning style
            (first day of class).

        2. Definitions of unfamiliar vocabulary (in your
            notebook).

        3. Three (3) two-to-three page learning essays and one
            (1) five-to-eight page activity analysis.

        4. One observational report on a field visit to an
            O.T. treatment setting.

        5. Two media information sheets.

        6. A plan for instructing a craft at the craft fair.

        7. Ten short-answer essays that appear on the quizzes
            and final exam.

    B. Writing Guidelines: For this course, you will be given
        formats to follow when writing reports, plans, and
        media information sheets.

        In writing the three learning essays and the activity
        analysis, please observe the following:

        1. All papers must be typed on white unlined paper and
            be double-spaced.

        2. All papers must have one-inch margins on top,
            bottom, and both sides.

3. Spelling and grammar are considered in the grading of papers.

C. Collection of Assignments: All written work is due on the date assigned, and points will be taken off for lateness. Be sure to check your syllabus for assignments on a daily basis.

D. Writing Outlines and Drafts: Even accomplished writers work in stages. You should do this too. Write an outline of your paper before writing the paper itself. Write more than one draft of your paper. It will improve with the second writing. Your instructor will go over this in class. BE SURE TO PROOFREAD ALL WRITTEN WORK BEFORE SUBMITTING IT.

E. Important Points: Because you will be using your writing skills in your future career, the following are important to keep in mind:

1. Clarity. All writing submitted must show thoughtfulness of organization and development of ideas. In the essays, you should begin with a clear statement of topic, develop your ideas through several paragraphs, and end with a clear summary statement.

2. Conciseness. Wherever possible, be direct and brief in your statements. If you repeat or paraphrase a point, you should give more details or examples. It is better to write a short paragraph that is clear and concisely written than several longer paragraphs that are wordy, repetitive, and unclear.

3. Proofreading. Before you hand in any written work (this includes exams), be sure to proofread it. Look out for the kinds of errors you know you've had trouble with before. Use your dictionary, if necessary. (Dictionaries are not permitted in exams.)

4. Writing Errors. In your writing assignments, pay particular attention to the following errors. I will use the indicated conventional symbols in marking errors on your work.

SYMBOL	MEANING	EXPLANATION	ILLUSTRATION
Frag	fragment	The sentence is incomplete.	I hear the wind. Blowing in the trees. Frag
RO	run-on sentence	Two complete sentences are run together without suitable connectors or end marks.	This media is done bilaterally it can be done with one hand also. RO
Agr	agreement	Subject and verb do not agree in number.	He go to the movies. Agr
Sp	spelling	A word is spelled incorrectly.	It's allright. Sp
Vb	verb	There is an error in the verb.	He was suppose to go. Vb
Cap	capital	A capital letter is required.	I study spanish. Cap

II. Oral/Aural Activities and General Guidelines

Health professionals must be able to communicate clearly with their patients and with each other. In order to help you develop and refine your oral communication skills, a variety of speaking (oral) and listening (aural) activities are included in this course.

A. Assignments: The oral/aural activities in which you are expected to participate are:

1. Question-and-answer dialogues in the weekly lecture session.

2. Laboratory discussions twice a week (see guides on p. 114 and p. 115).

3. Presentation of a craft to the rest of the class (see guide on p. 113).

4. Instruction of a craft at the craft fair.

5. Attending to the important points of the lectures (see lecture guide questions on p. 98).

6. Attending to the laboratory discussions (see guide on p. 115)

B. Guidelines: In each of these activities you should be working toward the following goals:

1. Speaking clearly and with appropriate volume.

2. Organizing your presentation in a logical fashion.

3. Eliminating irrelevant details.

4. Sticking to the subject.

5. Using standard English and avoiding slang.

6. Listening critically.

During the term the class will attend to the above areas by the techniques of mirroring and labeling--to be explained.

In addition, your instructor may ask that you make a carbon copy of your notes, to be handed in. This will help your instructor see how well you are listening to and recording the main points of the lectures.

III. Reading Activities and General Guidelines

A. Reading: You have two main texts for this course. Health Professional/Patient Interaction by Ruth Purtilo provides background for the lectures and for some of the writing assignments. The book discusses many personal, social, and ethical issues that concern health care workers. This book is abbreviated as HPPI on your syllabus.
     The second book is Craft Techniques in Occupational Therapy by the Department of the Army. This book describes the tools and materials used in craft activities, gives step-by-step explanations of how to do the crafts, and offers ideas on how to use these crafts with patients. This book is abbreviated as CTOT on your syllabus.
     Other readings can be found in the packet of handouts that your instructor will distribute. Specific reading assignments are listed on your course syllabus. It is essential that you do the assigned reading before coming to class.
     Your instructor will preview both of the major texts with you within the first week. This will acquaint you with the major features of the books and will give you some hints on how to use them.

B. Reading Guide Questions and Use of Cue Words: Guide questions for the assigned readings begin on p. 28 of this guide. The purpose of these questions is to help you focus on and remember those aspects of the readings that are most important for this course. You should write answers to these questions in your own words, based on your understanding of the information in the texts. Your instructor will review your answers periodically.

The readings in CTOT are extremely important to your successful performance in lab activities. Be sure to answer the guide questions for these readings before coming to class. You will find this a great advantage in learning each craft in the lab, as you will already be familiar with the tools, processes, and materials used.

Guide statements and questions begin with certain cue words that identify the type of information required. These cue words are explained as follows:

CUE WORDS

define	to give the distinguishing characteristics of
list identify name state	to give a series of
describe	to give details in sensory words
illustrate	to give examples
explain why	to give reasons for
explain how	to give details in the process of
analyze	to examine in detail
compare	to give similarities and differences
contrast	to give differences
delineate	to give details of, to outline precisely

C. Vocabulary:

1. Define each listed word you do not already know in your own way. Use the dictionary, if necessary, but do not copy the dictionary definition.

2. Use your dictionary to determine how each word is pronounced. Say each word out loud to yourself several times. Read aloud the sentence in which each word appears in your text.

3. You may wish to list any other unfamiliar words you encounter in your reading. Follow steps 1 and 2 above for each of these words. This is a very important habit to develop; if you do not understand the meaning of the words used, you will not understand the readings.

4.   Your written definitions need not be handed in.
Words from these lists will be on the exams,
however.

Course: Freshman Advisory Seminar (Seminar is offered by
Department of Student Services and passage is taken from the
LaGuardia Handbook, LaGuardia Community College, the City
University of New York, 1981-82, p. 6)

What is ISR?

ISR stands for "integrated skills reinforcement." ISR is a
special program designed to help you use and continue to develop
your reading, writing, and oral communication skills.

What is an ISR Learning Guide?

An ISR learning guide contains a series of activities and
exercises (such as reading and writing guided assignments) which
are designed to help you improve your basic skills so that you
can succeed at LaGuardia.

How Will ISR Help You?

By completing your assignments, you will learn about the college
and acquire information about the various policies and
procedures. You will also learn other skills to help you perform
more effectively in your courses (i.e., study skills, test-taking
strategies, etc.). This guide will help you learn more about
your future career as well as gain a better understanding of
yourself. Bring it to class every week, along with the Freshman
Seminar Curriculum, the Student Handbook, and the College
Bulletin.

General Course Requirements

Reading Assignments: For this seminar you will be reading from
the College Bulletin, the Student Handbook, and the Freshman
Seminar Curriculum. You should read each chapter in these books.
Each week before coming to class you should read the section we
will be discussing. If you do not understand some of the material, underline it in the book. If you have a question, write it
in the margin. When class meets again, be sure to ask for an
explanation of what you did not understand or your questions. If
your English is limited, try to ask a friend, a family member, or
another student to read and explain the material to you so that
you may better understand the information in these books. It is
very important that you know the information in order to be a
successful student at LaGuardia.

Previewing: Previewing is a skill which helps you obtain
information before you actually begin reading, by looking over
the sections and main features (e.g., glossary, headings, key
words). I will preview the Student Handbook and the College
Bulletin in class. You will preview the other materials
distributed (e.g., Basic Skills Handbook, Cooperative Education).

Reading Guide Questions: For each reading assignment, I have
developed focus questions and guide questions. Focus questions
will help you to think about the topic and listen attentively in
class. They will promote class discussion. Guide questions are
designed to guide you to gain an understanding of important
issues or information in your reading assignments. You should
answer the questions in your own words, using the information you
have just read in the section of the curriculum or the books. By
answering the guide questions you will be prepared for and can
participate in class discussions.
     Special cue words will appear in each guide question. These
cue words will help you answer the questions. They will also be
used in class discussion. It is important that you understand
their meanings. The following is a list of these specific cue
words and their definitions:

CUE WORDS

paraphrase	to restate in your own words
define	to state the meaning of; to list the distinguishing components of
describe	to give details
explain	to give reasons for
illustrate	to give examples of
interpret	to give your personal perceptions, thoughts, or ideas
analyze	to examine critically part by part
compare/contrast	to give similarities or differences
agree/disagree	to consent or differ in opinion
synthesize	to combine the parts into a whole

Writing Assignments: For this seminar, your writing assignments
will consist of answering the questions for each session of the
curriculum. In addition, you will write one paragraph during the
first session and one paragraph during the ninth session.
     A worksheet has been designed to help you obtain information
on your future career. You must write the answer to the questions on this worksheet. I will collect your assignments
throughout the quarter.

Oral Communication: In this seminar, class participation is very important. If there is something you do not understand, let me know either in Spanish or in English and I will explain it to you. The more you participate, the more productive and satisfying the course will be for you. The seminar will be conducted in English to help you develop your oral and aural skills in English.

Oral skill is the ability to speak thoughtfully when interacting with one another, either in discussions or when asking or responding to questions.

Aural skill is the ability to listen and understand what is being communicated. It is important that you learn to listen critically to both content (what we say) and form (how we say it). When we listen for content, we will be listening to whether the correct response is given to a question, whether the person stays on the topic or gives reactions or opinions rather than facts or details. When we listen for form, we will be listening for volume, pronunciation, and grammar (using words correctly).

In this seminar you will have an opportunity to practice your English. I want to encourage your participation. Do not feel limited if you do not know the words in English. If you have trouble pronouncing a word, I will say it and you can repeat it. You can also state your thought in Spanish, and I will repeat it in English and you can restate your thought in English.

Student Information Form

In order for me to get to know you better and for me to be of help to you, I have prepared an information sheet that I would appreciate your completing at home and bringing back to our second session. If you have any questions, I will answer them at that time.

FRESHMAN SEMINAR

STUDENT INFORMATION FORM

Date _____

Freshman Seminar _____

Name _____ Soc. Sec. # _____

Address _____

_____ Zip Code _____

Phone # _____ Business _____

Date of Birth _____ Single _____ Married _____ #Children _____

Your major here _____

Previous college or technical institute attended _____

_____

Credits completed there _____

Has an official copy of that transcript been forwarded to

LaGuardia? _____

If so, when? _____

Are you presently employed? _____

If so, where? _____

Job title _____ Hrs. per wk. _____

Career goal _____

How sure are you of this career goal? (circle one)

           not sure   pretty sure   very sure

What do you expect to do immediately after graduation?

     Transfer to 4-yr. college _____ Work full time _____

     Work and study _____ Undecided _____

List the courses that you will be taking this quarter

_____   _____

_____   _____

_____   _____

When you registered, you received a computerized sheet with your
first-quarter program. This sheet is called your Degree
Requirement Checklist. On the bottom of that sheet is a list of
Basic Skills courses. From that list, check the Basic Skills
courses that are a requirement for you:

CSE 096 _____   ENG 099 _____

CSE 097 _____   MAT 098 _____

CSE 098 _____   MAT 099 _____

CSE 099 _____   ESL 096 _____

CSE 103 _____   ESL 097 _____

HUC 098 _____   ESL 098 _____

HUC 099 _____   ESL 099 _____

ENG 098 _____

If you do not know which Basic Skills course you must take, go to
the Registrar's Office, Room 104, and speak to someone there.
They will give you the results of your placement test and tell
you which Basic Skills course you must take.

Index